Buildings and Places in Welsh History

Buildings and Places in Welsh History

A New History of Wales

Edited by

H. V. Bowen

Gomer

Picture Acknowledgements:
Unless otherwise credited, all the photographs in this book are reproduced
with the kind permission of Media Wales and the *Western Mail*.

Published in 2013 by
Gomer Press, Llandysul, Ceredigion, SA44 4JL

ISBN 978 1 84851 660 1

A CIP record for this title is available from the British Library.
© Individual essays: the contributors, 2013
© The Collection: History Research Wales and Gomer Press, 2013

History Research Wales asserts its moral right under
the Copyright, Designs and Patents Act, 1988
to be identified as author of this work.

This book is published with the financial support of the
Welsh Books Council.

Printed and bound in Wales at
Gomer Press, Llandysul, Ceredigion

Contents

Contents (*continued*)

Preface

History is about people. It is about what they did, why they did it, and what the consequences were. As historians we try to make sense of it all by recovering, analysing, and explaining what people in the past have left behind. It was primarily people who animated and shaped the world around them, and individually and collectively their actions are what makes the past so interesting and of great importance to us all. Not surprisingly, historical biographies are piled high in book shops. And, as was revealed by the response to our last volume on heroes and villains in Welsh history, it seems that we all like assessing the strengths and weaknesses of those who lived in the past.

But history is also all about place. This is because places provide the context for all human actions, and like our ancestors we are all shaped by our environment: where we live, work, and visit. Some places are formed by the natural environment, and others are created by us for specific reasons. As a result, places can be beautiful and enjoyable, functional and mundane, challenging and dangerous, safe and secure, interesting and thought-provoking.

Some places change rapidly; others seem barely to alter at all over the centuries; and yet others again disappear completely from view. Places that were once important lose their significance and meaning, while other places rise briefly to prominence because of a particular event or episode. We might visit these places every day; we might only ever see them once in our lives.

Some places are instantly forgettable; others leave a deep and vivid impression upon our consciousness. Places can give us a sense of rootedness, identity, and civic pride, but they can also be the cause of misery, despair, and humiliation. In short, place matters in history, and for each and every one of us different places have made us all what we are as individuals, communities, and a nation.

It is for these reasons that buildings and places in Welsh history will be discussed in the third volume of essays to be published by Gomer in association with the *Western Mail* and History Research Wales. This remains a unique enterprise. Nowhere else in the world does a national newspaper give over space to a group of academics so that they can write 2,500 words a day for a month on whatever subject they want, without any editorial interference whatsoever. It is these words, and some outstanding pictures, that are now published in this book.

Why do the historians write these essays for public rather than academic audiences? We write these essays because it is vital that those in our universities communicate their thoughts, insights, and very latest research findings beyond the academy. This is a process of engagement that contributes to the making of a vibrant, confident, and intelligent nation that is secure in its knowledge of where it has come from and where it might be going.

As in the previous two volumes, we want to encourage readers to think critically about Welsh history. We don't wish to provoke controversy for controversy's sake but we do want to challenge myths and misconceptions about the significance of selected places and buildings. And in bringing our latest research findings to readers we want to take them to the cutting-edge of current debate. This can only be done in the essay form, where the author has the space to develop an argument and support it with detail and evidence.

We certainly won't be recounting an old-fashioned story of Wales, because good history is not about telling well-known tales. The past is a complex and difficult place that can't be easily packaged and explained. There are many rough edges and awkward bits, and they need a combination of expertise and extended commentary to make them comprehensible. Even then, there will always be much to disagree about, and this is where debate comes in as the essential ingredient for good history.

Nobody owns the past, least of all academic historians, and no-one has a monopoly in terms of delivering the history of a nation, state, community, or place. For at the end of the day, historians only speak for themselves, and wherever possible they should be challenged to justify their choices, explanations, and interpretations. In the essays that follow, leading historians from across the Welsh universities will discuss some of the buildings and places that they think are important. We will be visiting some familiar places, and some that are unfamiliar or indeed unknown. We will explore Wales from the very top of Snowdon to the depths of the Brynglas tunnels on the M4 motorway. Along the way we will reflect on the importance of many of the places where Welsh history was made and, most importantly, is still being made.

As ever, I wish to thank Ceri Gould and Alan Edmunds of the Western Mail/ Media Wales. Their interest in, and support for, Welsh history is reflected in the content of their newspaper and this helps to ensure that modern Wales remains firmly connected to, and understands, its past. It is a pleasure to work with them. I thank Ceri Wyn Jones of Gwasg Gomer for his patience, support, and good humour. It is good fun working with him on these books. Special thanks go to Tony Woolway, the Picture Librarian at Media Wales, who goes far beyond the call of duty in helping us to produce these books. And, on this occasion, I am indebted to Peter Wakelin of the Royal Commission for the Ancient and Historical Monuments of Wales for not only writing a thought-provoking introduction but also facilitating access to the Commission's wonderful collection of photographs. Most of all, I am indebted to my academic colleagues who take time out from their busy lives to write interesting, challenging essays on a wide range of subjects. Diolch yn fawr iawn.

Huw Bowen, Swansea, April 2013

St David's Cathedral

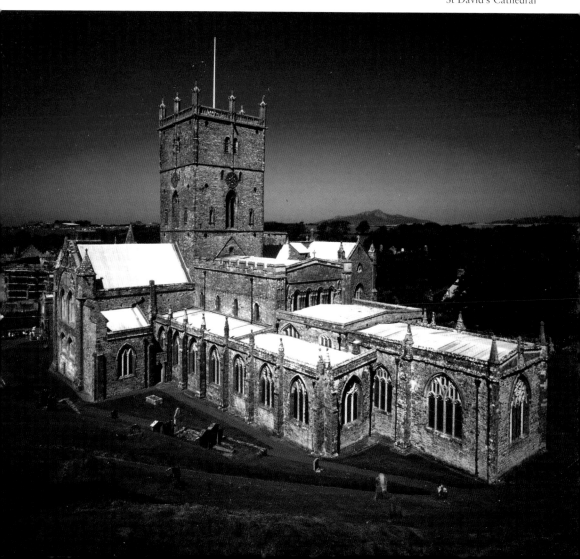

Introduction:
Messages from the Past

Peter Wakelin

The essays in this book on buildings and places in Welsh history speak eloquently for the way in which our surroundings connect us with people who have gone before.

I was hit personally by this ability to link between the generations when my aunt died, aged 92, the last of my parents' generation. I wished I had asked her about all sorts of things when I had the chance. But after her funeral I took a detour past the home where we used to visit her when I was small, and seeing the house again evoked powerful memories.

If I recall the many places where my family lived across the generations, they all have things to tell me, not just about personal identity but about big themes in 20th-century Welsh history too. They tell me about mining and iron-making roots in the Rhymney valley, about how quickly money could be made and lost between the wars, the explosive growth of Cardiff, movements of population back and forth across the English border, and burgeoning life-opportunities following the transformations of health and education.

Over half a century ago, W. G. Hoskins wrote in *The Making of the English Landscape* that the 'landscape itself, to those who know how to read it aright, is the richest historical record we possess'. If buildings and places are historical documents, they have one great advantage over any others: they are there at every corner to challenge our assumptions and remind us that people once lived differently. Even the most modern and the most apparently ordinary buildings have something to say about the people who made them. Evidence is wherever you look – even in your own home, school or workplace.

My colleagues and I at the Royal Commission on the Ancient and Historical Monuments of Wales, the national archive and investigation body for Wales's built heritage, have the luck to spend our time studying buildings and landscapes of all types, from prehistory to the present. We undertake research and look after documentation produced by ourselves and others in the National Monuments Record of Wales so that we can provide information, up-to-date interpretations and advice to underpin the management of the historical environment and help people study history.

A huge number of people today find that taking interest in their surroundings historically opens different ways of seeing, a daily doorway into a kind of parallel universe of the past. Some people denigrate this as a middle-class pursuit, but that is patronising; in fact the interest transcends all backgrounds and all walks of life. Nearly everyone sees a value in it.

In still-used buildings and landscapes layered with modern-day activities, past and present coexist. There can be a sense of revelation when you first start to read the clues, like messages from a lost world, in the same way that gaining a little knowledge of botany transforms a walk in the woods or knowing some astronomy helps you see the night sky not just as points of light but planets, nebulas and the evidence of the Big Bang. Opening your eyes to history makes the whole world look different.

If you live in Cardiff, for example, you can walk out of your house and see how land ownership in the 19th century is still visible. At that time, if you wanted to build on Bute estate land you had to follow the Marquis's Gothic-based plan; but if you were on Tredegar land the style had to be Italianate. And so if you walk from Tredegarville to Roath you cross an architectural rift, and you can still feel the tremors of the grandees' rivalry.

ESSAYS IN THE BOOK

In this collection of essays some of Wales's best historians have chosen examples of buildings and places that convey historical significance – for them, and for the rest of us, they hope. There are important distinctions between 'history' and 'heritage'. The pursuit of history is about striving for understanding, while the processes of heritage are primarily concerned with celebrating and utilising assets. These essays are determinedly about the former. They have not been written to praise their subjects or promote tourism and amenity but with an eye to what sites and buildings tell us, good or bad. True historians will never agree to the interpretation of our past becoming nostalgic or tourism-driven. As Robin Barlow's essay on Mametz Wood reminds us, even episodes as horrific as the First World War must be remembered, and be examined with forensic care not sentiment or jingoism. History is being made today as well as signifying the past of long ago, and it's on the doorstep as well as in buzzing honey-pots like Tintern Abbey or Cardiff Castle.

Tintern Abbey

Some of these essays represent the deep past, such as lakes sacred to people of the Bronze Age (explored by Raimund Karl), the Cistercian abbey of Strata Florida (considered by David Austin), and the tomb of Rhys ap Maredudd (Madeleine Gray). Chris Williams has written about Snowdon, somewhere that seems timeless but is layered with changing human relationships through the centuries. Other places stand for much more recent history, even for history being made right now. Huw Bowen interprets football grounds, Andy Croll examines the resort at Barry Island. Martin Johnes has chosen the M4: it may not be 'heritage' but has any construction had greater impact on Wales in the last forty years? Andrew Edwards looks at the Senedd in Cardiff Bay, the recent, signature piece of architecture that we very nearly didn't build to express the aspirations of the nation.

My own historical fascination is with the industrial revolution, which can be said to be the first time that Wales had a world-wide impact. The nation's industrial sites and buildings rank in universal value with the remains of Renaissance Italy and Ancient Greece. In that sense, it's no surprise that they are well represented in this book, yet just a generation ago they probably would

13

not have been, nor deemed worth preservation – evidence that perceptions of value are constantly evolving.

Industrial-era Merthyr Tydfil is discussed by Chris Evans. Merthyr is still surely the most under-appreciated of great historic towns anywhere. It was the world's first true iron or steel town, setting the pattern for others from Pittsburgh to Donetsk. If you take a walk around it you can still detect how competing iron companies fought for land, how streets began on lines of railways, how terraces of houses had to fit in spaces left between the works and slag heaps. Other industrial-era essays discuss the planned town of Tredegar, Penallta colliery, Talerddig railway cutting, and a relic of Welsh industrial influence overseas, Washburn Street cemetery in Scranton, Pennsylvania. Places like these pose tough questions about harsh lives and social failure as well as representing innovation and achievement.

LOST HERITAGE

We have lost an astonishing number of industrial sites and buildings over the last two generations, and some historically important sites continue to decay. In the 1960s and 1970s the breathtakingly lace-like piers of Crumlin Viaduct were torn down and outstanding elements of Merthyr's heritage such as the Triangle workers' housing and the Iron Bridge were cleared away. Luckily, thousands of disappearing sites have been recorded and the evidence has been retained in the National Monuments Record, ensuring that not all of their historical value is lost.

Brynmawr Rubber Factory, the first post-war building in Britain to be listed, was demolished a few years ago, Trawsfynydd's nuclear reactor houses are being dismantled, the Glyn Pits beam engines hang on in dereliction and Treforest tinplate works is crumbling. But the former passion to clear any trace of industrial grime and strife has largely given way to a more mature appreciation that our history is our history, pretty or not. The Royal Commission played key roles in two successful industrial nominations to join places like Stonehenge and Venice on the prestigious World Heritage List – Blaenavon Industrial Landscape (inscribed in 2000) and Pontcysyllte Aqueduct and Canal (2010). Work is underway to nominate the Welsh slate industry, with its remarkable evidence of hard labour and technical resourcefulness in tough environments.

There have been some near misses. Blaenavon ironworks, now the heart of the World Heritage Site, was once due for reclamation. Distinctive features of Cardiff Bay such as the graving docks and timber signal platforms were to be cleared away in initial plans for waterfront development. The buildings of

Caernarfon Castle: history, heritage and controversy, all in one building and place

Swansea's Hafod copperworks are being rescued after years of lingering on the edge of total loss.

Industrial sites are not the only ones at risk. Iron Age promontory defences are being damaged by coastal erosion. The earthworks of medieval moated sites get ploughed out. Great mansions like Edwinsford in Carmarthenshire have continued their gradual decay for generations. Accelerating closure is threatening even churches, the most-hallowed traditional focal points of our communities. The Royal Commission continues to record historical buildings and archaeological sites in danger, whether to support future conservation or to retain some remembrance of them alongside evidence of thousands of others that have been lost already. Hence, archaeological features in the uplands, increasingly vulnerable to the erosion of peat with accelerating climate change, are being identified as fast as possible. Chapels, often regarded as the national architecture of Wales, are the subject of a Wales-wide study of more than six thousand that have existed. Even as they continue closing at a rate of one a week, detailed research is throwing up fascinating stories of prolific chapel architects and the aspirations of congregations, and charting the rise and fall of chapel-building, denominations and styles, so that we will understand our nonconformist history and remaining chapels much better, even though many hundreds, even thousands, will have gone.

WELL-BEING

Is our interest in historic buildings and sites a luxury? We can't care for all of them, especially when resources are few and far between, but collecting information, and developing understanding, costs almost nothing by comparison. This can help us make informed choices about preservation. Even more importantly, though, it contributes to our well-being as a nation. Any society that does not embrace its history or that values only comfortable heritage is like someone with selective memory or dementia, steadily losing identity and capability – think of the totalitarian regimes that airbrush the opposition from history or the tourist paradises that permit only the most attractive history to be revealed. Wales cannot afford to be a society like that.

While few people give special thought to the 'uses' of history, we say things every day that show we use it all the time. We think by reference to the past, saying 'Get a sense of perspective', 'Has it always been like this?' or 'How did we do it last time?'. The past challenges our assumptions too. If you wander the hills above Blaenavon you can see how men, women and children laboured twelve-hour shifts in bitter cold to move a mountain – and you respect their toughness and feel glad of where we are today. We gain similar perspective on our own lives by looking at the one-room cottages of poor rural families, or thinking how Iron Age slaves must have heaved all a hill fort's water up a half-mile ascent.

Exploring local history brings communities together and fosters belonging, as many history groups know well, whether long-established county antiquarian societies, well-heeled village groups or Communities First partnerships. The number of such groups is astounding – there are thousands around Wales; forty in the Swansea valley alone.

Many people find visiting buildings and places a motivation for getting out and about in ways that support their health, whether finding interest for a stroll around their neighbourhood, visiting heritage attractions or hiking up hillsides to see mines, cairns and camps. With history especially popular among older people, this activity is important, especially for those who might otherwise be isolated, because it gives them opportunities for exercise, enjoyment, companionship and relaxation.

INSPIRATION

In L. P. Hartley's phrase, 'The past is a foreign country; they do things differently there.' Architects have looked to historic buildings for ideas and references since the Renaissance. Students at the Welsh School of Architecture recently did a group project on the Heads of the Valleys that began with finding out about the past – its successes and mistakes – before making proposals for the future. Similarly, the owners of historic buildings, conservation officers and community groups find out about previous conservation works and comparable sites before deciding on the approaches they are going to take.

It may seem counter-intuitive, but scientists and technologists, too, gain inspiration from looking at the past. For example, they can revisit sustainable methods used in historic watermills and windmills, cottages built from local materials or ironworks that recycled gas. The Institution of Civil Engineers has a proud record of cataloguing and studying historical structures so as to make good decisions in the future.

The past has always inspired visual art, films, drama, poetry and prose – whether Romantic-era poets and painters responding to ruins, contemporary artists connecting with places that have complex meanings, schoolchildren working creatively in their communities, or the continuing appetite for making period drama. The conceptual artist Tim Davies used historical bridges and war memorials as points of departure for his work when he represented Wales at the Venice Biennale. A series of poets responded to images in the National Monuments Record for the Royal Commission's centenary in 2008. The historical environment also inspires tourists to come to Wales, where eighty per cent of the most visited attractions are heritage sites. It's a truism, too, that places people want to visit are places where they want to live, and places people want to live are places where people want to invest.

WISDOM AND VALUES

Our relationships with the historic environment are subtle. People in the past may be role models or signal monsters. A few of the children who learn about how Thomas Telford dared to throw a suspension bridge across the Menai Strait will be inspired to think all things are possible, and those who trace clues to the Swansea Blitz around the townscape may grow up with a better grasp of the reality of war.

Having an authentic grip on the past strengthens our identity and distinctiveness, as individuals, families, communities and nation. Confidence can come from historically-informed perceptions of our places, for example, from appreciating that iron towns like Merthyr at their height were among the most dynamic places in the world, teeming with initiative, skill and invention. Can knowing this prompt questions for today, such as what were the conditions that made them so vibrant, and how can we revive equivalent ambition?

The past is rich in lessons. The evidence of past climate change can bring home the reality of change today – whether it be traces of farming in what later became barren uplands or the sand dunes that overwhelmed medieval settlements like Kenfig in great storms. Looking at the impact of past immigrants fosters understanding of the complex mix of people that has made Wales what it is, and prompts tolerance today: you can see evidence of influxes from Rome, Scandinavia, Normandy; Italians who built coffee shops in the Depression, German émigrés escaping Nazi persecution who set up factories at Treforest, or Cardiff's long-established Islamic communities who founded some of the first mosques in Britain.

FINDING OUT MORE

We can be in touch with the past by reading books like this one, by exploring free online resources like those for 100,000 Welsh sites and buildings on www.coflein.gov.uk, by watching television programmes such as *Hidden Histories* and *The Story of Wales*, and of course by exploring places for ourselves, whether iconic sites or our own neighbourhoods.

Just observing is a great starting point. The buildings and places right on your doorstep have stories to tell about everyday lives in the past as well as major events. Detailed study tells you even more, which is why archaeologists, building historians and other specialists investigate and share results. Even ancient archaeological sites are still being found – each year the Welsh Archaeological Trusts, independent researchers and the Royal Commission discover hundreds that had been lost from memory.

W. G. Hoskins said the landscape is a document, provided we know how to read it aright. The essays in this book help us learn to do exactly that.

Further reading
Peter Wakelin and Ralph Griffiths (eds), *Hidden Histories: Discovering the Heritage of Wales* (2008)
The National Monuments Record in Aberystwyth is the biggest visual collection in Wales, with over 2 million photographs, 125,000 drawings and details of 100,000 sites and buildings. It can be explored at www.coflein.gov.uk

1

THE HIMALAYAN GIANT – SNOWDON/YR WYDDFA

Chris Williams

In December 1940, during one of the bleakest phases of the Second World War, the mountaineer Frank Smythe left the bomb-damaged city of Liverpool to seek peace and serenity amidst the hills of Snowdonia. In 1933 Smythe had gone as high on Everest as any man before the Swiss expedition of 1952 (with the possible exception of George Mallory and Andrew Irvine in 1924). Walking above the Ogwen valley, a Spitfire 'whirled through the pass' at his feet and, a few days later, on Snowdon's razor-sharp Crib Goch ridge, Smythe reflected that 'there was a silence reminiscent not of a British countryside but of the plateaux of Central Asia'. 'Was it possible', he asked, 'that the greatest war of all time was raging? It seemed incredible. ...Never had war seemed more insane'.

I suspect that those of you who also have enjoyed the solitude and splendour of Eryri/Snowdonia will understand what Frank Smythe meant. For him the contrast was stark: between the Luftwaffe raining bombs from the air on a city not far distant and the mountains standing unmoved by the latest chapter of human folly. Subsequent generations have been more fortunate: the high hills have been refuges not from enemy action but from the frustrations and pace of modern living. And, for those who stop 'to look to't, think on't', they remain reminders of, ultimately, the fleeting nature of humankind's acquaintance with the planet.

Snowdon (never 'Mount' Snowdon!) is the grandest reminder of them all. At 3,560 feet or 1,085 metres above sea level, it stands taller than any other mountain in England, let alone in Wales. Geologists suggest its rocks were formed more than 450 million years ago, during the Ordovician period. It has sported its names for at least the last millennium. We find it referenced in the

Anglo-Saxon Chronicle in 1095, and in 1188 Gerald of Wales titles it Snaudune – literally 'snow hill' in old English. However, the mightily prosaic nature of the English name (it has the advantage of being easy for visitors to pronounce, unlike neighbouring Elidir Fawr or Carnedd Llywelyn) is revealed by contrast with the Welsh title, first recorded in 1198 – the much grander 'Yr Wyddfa'.

YR WYDDFA

Yr Wyddfa means 'the burial mound' or 'tomb', and legend has it that the mountain's summit marks the grave of Rhita Gawr – a giant who liked to kill kings and make cloaks from their beards. On the whole commentators have not thought such qualities admirable, but an exception was made by Edward Williams, the stonemason, bard, patriot and fantasist better known as Iolo Morganwg (1747–1826). Iolo approved of lovely Rhita – seeing him as a proto-republican (which may be stretching a point) and an advocate of international peace (though I'm not quite sure *how* Iolo squared that bardic circle)!

Some writers argue that Rhita met his match, eventually, at the hands of King Arthur. But Arthur is more commonly associated with suffering a mortal wound at the hands of regular-sized enemies, in the latter stages of a battle that took place on the flanks of the Snowdon massif. Bwlch y Saethau – the pass of the arrows – the col that separates the summit of Yr Wyddfa from the double peaks of Lliwedd, is named after the episode, and until the 19th century there was a large cairn – Carnedd Arthur – located nearby.

The most romantic legend suggests that the stricken Arthur was taken by his comrades to be buried in a cave on the thousand foot rock wall of the north face of Lliwedd. There he waits, with hundreds of his warriors, ready to respond to the call of his people. Once a shepherd strayed into the cave, thought to be in Slanting Gully, and accidentally rang a bell which awoke the Arthurian troglodytes. Hastily he reassured the *llanciau Eryri* ('Snowdonian lads') that they were not yet needed, and they returned to their slumbers. Unhappily, he was never again able to locate the site.

THE MAN-EATING OTTER

An equally plausible story is attached to Glaslyn, the lake directly beneath the mountain's summit. This is reputedly the home of the afanc, an aquatic creature which, according to those who have seen it, is a cross between an otter (some say a beaver – Gerald of Wales wrote of beavers on the river Teifi in the 12th century) and a crocodile. Next time you ascend the mountain from the east see if you can spot one splashing in the shallows!

A pause for breath

USE AND ABUSE

Snowdon, then, is rooted in the Welsh past, even if some of the stories associated with it should be handled with care. It existed before anyone had thought of 'Wales' and it will exist long after 'Wales' has ceased to be relevant to the problems all humankind will surely face. But it would be wrong to think of it as an unsullied, static landscape, for clearly human action has made a difference to its surface and to how we look upon it.

Agriculturally, as with much of upland Wales, it has been a terrain where sheep graze and wild goats wander, but where the elevation and rainfall deter the cultivation of arable crops.

21

Industrially its history is more surprising. Like many mountains, far from its features being entirely 'natural', it has been scathed, marked and changed to suit our wants and needs. The waters of the aforementioned Glaslyn ('green lake') are tinted by copper ore. Various copper mining enterprises tried their luck on Snowdon's slopes, including the Brittania (yes, it did have two 't's and one 'n') Copper Mine, which closed in 1926.

Next to Llyn Teyrn (a mile from Pen-y-Pass at the head of Nant Peris) was once a barracks built to house up to a hundred copper miners. And the causeway that crosses the northern end of Llyn Llydaw was built by the Cwmdyle Rock and Green Lake Copper Mining Company, using 6,000 cubic yards of waste rock from its mining operations.

Before all the copper mines closed the mountain was serving a new need: in 1906 the Cwm Dyli hydro-electric power station was built, carrying water down from Llyn Llydaw to Afon Glaslyn at the head of Nant Gwynant. Its moment in the spotlight came over 90 years later, when it was a location featured in the James Bond film *The World is Not Enough*, starring Pierce Brosnan, Robbie Coltrane, Robert Carlyle, Sophie Marceau, Patrick Malahide etc.

It's difficult to believe that, today, they wouldn't bury the pipeline that is clearly visible from the A498 running south to Beddgelert, but it was only in 1951 that Snowdonia gained National Park status and such environmental depredations were more tightly controlled.

Real-life James Bonds (Royal Marine Commandos) trained on Snowdon during the Second World War, and the military connection goes back earlier, to 1827, when the Royal Engineers built the first cairn on the mountain's summit as part of an ordnance survey.

SNOWDON'S POLITICS

Welsh, rather than British soldiers, have long used Snowdon's cwms and cols to their advantage. The Welsh historian Sir John Lloyd argued that 'the fastnesses of Eryri ...have at every period played a crucial part in the history of Wales', offering 'a refuge and retreat to discomfited peoples' and providing 'an ideal theatre for national resistance of invasion'. It is no accident that it was in Gwynedd that a tradition of independent Welsh statehood lasted longest, or that it is in the same area that both the speaking of Welsh and support for Welsh nationalist politics have been consistently the strongest.

Snowdon may never have enjoyed the vote, but its slopes have occasionally been courted by politicians. Most famously, in 1892, the four-time Prime Minister William Ewart Gladstone ascended the southern flank of the mountain as far as a large boulder (1000 feet above sea level and now marked with a plaque), where he addressed a very large crowd on 'the land question' in Wales. He was eighty-three years old at the time, and hanging on his every word was David Lloyd George (who would become Prime Minister himself a quarter of a century later) and his host, Sir Edward Watkin.

A young Lloyd George heard Gladstone's sermon on Snowdon in 1892

Watkin, originally from Salford in Lancashire, was Liberal MP for Hythe in Kent at the time, but had built a summer chalet in Nant Gwynant. He then financed the building of a path (which continues to bear his name) to allow his family and guests to walk direct from the chalet to the summit of Snowdon. With that success under his belt, Watkin went on to sponsor an early (and abortive) attempt to construct a tunnel under the English Channel to France.

HOW MAY I CLIMB THEE? LET ME COUNT THE WAYS

Most who come to Snowdon put aside their political and religious concerns, if only for a day. Their desire is, whether through their own effort or through that of the Snowdon Mountain Railway (established 1896), to reach the top – 'because it is there'. Today it is estimated that over half a million people a year make that journey on foot. They may do so by at least seven different routes: including the relatively straightforward 'yak' route starting alongside the railway in Llanberis; the long slog of the Rhyd-Ddu path which eventually treats you to a bird's eye view of the rock climbers' paradise of the Clogwyn Du'r Arddu cliffs; and the vertigo-inducing scrambling of the Snowdon Horseshoe. Some years ago I introduced a fellow-contributor to this volume to the adrenaline rush of the Crib Goch ridge. As we rested afterwards near the summit café (before the marvellous new building was opened) he decided that, on reflection, he would shelve his ambition of attempting Everest!

All modern walkers and climbers tread in the footsteps of previous generations. The first to reach the summit of Snowdon were, surely, shepherds, travellers, hunters and warriors, but it was only in 1639 that a botanist named Thomas Johnson made the earliest recorded ascent. In 1798 two enterprising clergymen, William Bingley and Peter Williams (no relation), scampered up the Eastern Terrace of Clogwyn Du'r Arddu in search of exotic flora, and thereby staked a claim for the first documented rock climb in British history.

By the early 19th century, tourist ascents of the mountain were regular enough to warrant a refreshment hut being erected (in 1838). Later this developed into a hotel offering overnight accommodation, much in the way of Alpine hostels. Local men and boys acted as guides and one could expect to encounter other parties en route.

ASHAMED TO BE ENGLISH

George Borrow celebrated reaching the summit in the company of his daughter Henrietta in 1854 by reciting Welsh poetry. A Welshman standing near asked if he was a Breton. Borrow replied, 'I wish I was, or anything but what I am, one of a nation amongst whom any knowledge save what relates to money-making ... is looked upon as a disgrace. I am ashamed to say that I am an Englishman.'

But it was the English, especially those from the public schools and Oxbridge, who pioneered the modern rock-climbing scene in Snowdonia. Basing themselves at the Pen-y-Gwryd and Pen-y-Pass hotels, they came in winter and at Easter, forming the Society of Welsh Rabbits (1870) and the Climbers' Club (1898) and tracing dozens of new routes on Snowdon and its neighbours. They included some of the brightest and best of their generation: the artist Duncan Grant, the writer Robert Graves, the economist John Maynard Keynes, the politician Charles Trevelyan, his historian brother George, and the three Huxley brothers – Julian, Aldous and Trevenen. As Professor R. Merfyn Jones has noted, 'Climbing in Wales was the regular pursuit of some of the most talented and creative representatives of the British intelligentsia'.

Many were also leading mountaineers as well as intellectuals: Geoffrey Winthrop Young (who in 1957 co-authored *Snowdon Biography* – how many mountains are the subject of biographies?); the athletic London Welshman O. G. (he claimed his initials stood for 'Only Genuine') Jones; Siegfried Herford, born in Aberystwyth and killed at Festubert in 1916; and George Mallory, who perished on Everest in 1924. It was the strong connection of the district with the history and tradition of British mountaineering that led members of the 1953 Everest expedition to test themselves and their equipment here prior to the successful ascent of the world's highest peak.

TOP OF THE WELSH WORLD

Many over the centuries, then, have admired Snowdon, be they Welsh or not. To the 17th-century cartographer John Speed, 'Snowdon-Hill' was a 'British Alp'. Charles Darwin, writing in 1835, confessed that to him the mountain

Sir Edmund Hillary's
signature is amongst
those scribbled on the
ceiling of the Everest
Room at Pen-y-gwryd
Hotel

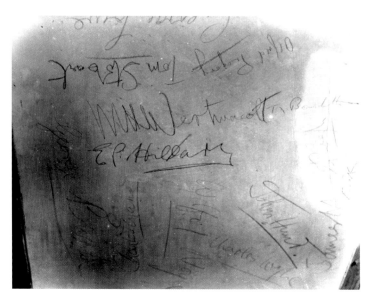

appeared 'much higher and much more beautiful than any peak in the Cordillera' of the Andes.

The numbers ascending in modern times show no sign of slackening. Some even seek to ascend by unorthodox means (the first time a motor car reached the summit was 1904). It would appear that the mountain exhibits an enduring popularity.

Is it the most important place in the history of Wales? In that it both predates and will postdate the history of what we know as Wales, it has a significant claim unrivalled by any man-made structure. Its own history is amazingly diverse. It is a site of powerful legends and entrancing myths. It is a symbol of Welsh resistance to English encroachment and conquest. It has provided a terrain from which some (such as industrialists and tourist entrepreneurs) have tried to prosper. In the last one hundred years it has been a place of secular pilgrimage for those seeking, through muscular effort and the careful calibration of skill against risk, to overcome the challenge of the vertical.

Ultimately, the selection of the most important place has to be a personal one. I have ascended Snowdon maybe half-a-dozen times, the first with my family (admittedly by train) when I was a boy, on all other occasions on foot, by different routes, with companions and alone, in sunshine and in snow. Living in South Wales, it is only the much closer (and lower) Pen y Fan, Corn Du and Cribyn that I have climbed more often.

I have slept close to the burial place of Rhita Gawr before a long day traversing all fourteen of the 'Welsh Three Thousands' from Snowdon in the

25

south to Foel Fras in the north. On four occasions I have dragged a reluctant body around the 26.2 miles of the Snowdonia Marathon, viewing the mountain from all angles before descending to a most welcome finish in Llanberis. Writing this, surrounded by guide books and maps, I feel that another ascent is overdue.

That, then, is the magic of Snowdon. It exerts a magnetic attraction, it makes your feet itch for your boots, because it is the highest peak, and in so many respects it is a beautiful and challenging mountain offering wonderful variety from every direction. You are unable to see all of Wales from its summit, but on a clear day you may feel you can.

Further Reading
Jim Perrin, *Snowdon: The Story of a Welsh Mountain* (2012)

The Snowdon train first reached the summit in 1896 and has been chugging away ever since

2

BEYOND CAERLEON AND CAMELOT – LODGE HILL

Ray Howell

Looming over the site of the Roman legionary fortress in Caerleon is the distinctive profile of Lodge Hill, today the location of a housing estate sprawling almost to the summit of the hill. Almost, but not quite. The top of the prominence is the scheduled site of an Iron Age hill fort, Lodge Hill Camp.

Roman Caerleon is a well-known heritage destination for visitors to Wales. The permanent base of the Second Augustan Legion for some two hundred years, Isca, as it was known to the Romans, was one of the most important military sites in Britain. Monuments like the amphitheatre, excavated barracks and fortress baths, and extensive surviving defensive walls have long been well known and recent excavations of a large port complex by Dr Peter Guest and his team have demonstrated that the site was even more important than we had previously believed.

Less well-known, but in some ways arguably as important, was the hill fort above the fortress. Lodge Hill had been abandoned well before construction of the Roman fortress began, but there was a time when it was a key element in a very different social system. At the local university, an interactive digital heritage trail for Roman Caerleon has recently been produced, including points like the hill fort, and, during the filming of the segment on top of the ramparts, one of the postgraduate students was dressed as a Roman centurion. The woods that cover much of the site are popular with ramblers and, as we were about to begin filming, an unsuspecting local man passed by, walking his dogs. Unsurprisingly, he did a double take and said, 'Bloody hell, you lot aren't coming back are you?' Three strides later, he stopped again, looked back and added, 'We'll bloody have you next time!'

That struck me as a quite refreshing exchange in the sense that our passer by clearly had a grasp of the nature of at least some of the history of the site. Lodge Hill was an important part of what can be described as a 'Silurian system', not in a geological sense but because it had once been a centre of the Silures, the Iron Age tribe of south-east Wales who fought the Romans for a quarter of a century in a bitter guerrilla war. Led first, at least in part, by the Catuvellaunian prince Caratacus and subsequently by their own clan-based hierarchy, the Silures achieved some notable military successes and even defeated a legion during protracted conflict which did not end until c75, when the governor Julius Frontinus ordered construction of Isca.

While there are many unanswered questions about the Silures and the nature of Silurian society, one of the things which is clear is that they built hill forts. Not all of these sites were on hills and there is ongoing archaeological debate about the extent to which they were forts. Nevertheless, they were certainly prominent features in the Iron Age landscape.

EXCAVATING THE SITE

Since these hill forts seem an obvious way to try to understand the Silures better, it is surprising how little archaeological work has been done on these sites. When we undertook limited excavations on Lodge Hill as a millennium-inspired project funded by the Charles Williams Educational Trust, it became, and remains, only the fifth of some 50 eastern, or Gwentian, hill forts to have been excavated. Our excavations were exploratory and limited. Nevertheless, we learned some very interesting things and demonstrated how a little excavation can go a long way in improving our understanding of Wales in the Iron Age.

For example, in the main open area excavation of the small inner enclosure of the hill fort, we found the footings of a roundhouse and a smaller sub-rectangular building. The small post-built rectangular structure had no hearth and seems to have been used for storage or some other ancillary purpose. It is good confirmatory evidence of an interesting aspect of Iron Age societies. The Silures, in common with other British tribes, chose to live in roundhouses. It was clearly a matter of choice because they knew perfectly well how to build rectangular buildings and often did in areas like the Gwent Levels. They used them to keep animals and for other purposes. However, when it came to themselves, as at Lodge Hill, they chose to live in roundhouses.

The artefacts were also interesting. The sherds of pottery, for example, gave us a picture of an active trading community. Some pots were locally made but others came from the Malvern Hills. Perhaps most interesting was

An aerial view of Caerleon, 1955

the briquetage, fragments of coarse conical salt containers. This material came from the Droitwich area and shows that salt was brought to the hill fort from the sixth century BC right up to the eve of the Roman conquest. The River Usk was an important trade route and we were able to show that Lodge Hill was a trading centre for much of the Iron Age.

Other finds included a La Tène brooch probably dating from the fourth century BC. The iron brooch appears to have an eight-coil spring mechanism for fastening. The appearance is deceptive. The apparent spring is really no more than a fashion accessory. Nevertheless, the craftsmanship is good and it complements a growing number of metalwork finds from across the area, including terrets and other horse trappings, which confirm that the Silures not only used horses but also wheeled vehicles. We didn't find horse fittings on site but the brooch is a nice addition to a catalogue of high quality metal work by the Silures. Appropriately, we also found iron slag, the waste material from iron production, on site.

Such results from the main excavation were good. So were the findings of other trenches including an exploration of the large main bank and associated ditch. This bit of the excavation was known within the digging team as 'Chad's ski slope' partly because it was supervised by Adrian Chadwick and partly because it was precipitous! Special care was certainly given to protective fencing to seal off the drop every night!

The bank and ditch investigation was challenging but the results were exciting. The massive stone and earth bank was supported by a timber lacing of vertical posts. There were several phases of construction and evidence that eventually the bank was revetted. Stone cladding might be the easiest way to describe what must have been visually very impressive to anyone approaching the site. Of particular interest was a collapse deposit, where the revetment seemed to have been pulled down, suggesting deliberate slighting of the defences. Sherds of Roman pottery give a good clue as to who may have been doing the slighting. It seems that the Roman army didn't want a still potentially occupied stronghold overlooking their fortress so they pulled down part of the defences.

An artist's impression of the Roman fortress

The third main trench investigated what today is the narrow entrance into the hill fort. It is an odd entrance with a ramp leading in. This ramp cuts through the banks and fills the ditches, making a nonsense of the Iron Age defences. For this and other reasons we thought this might be a late development and excavation confirmed that it was indeed a late re-cut. How late is difficult to say given the lack of finds but we concluded that it had been built late in the history of the site, possibly even in the post-Roman period.

RECCCUPATION

Reoccupation is an important theme on Lodge Hill and other regional hill forts. The Roman army left Caerleon in about AD270 and Cardiff became the military centre for this part of the world. However, recent excavations have confirmed that people were still living in and near the fortress in Caerleon with new structures going up in close proximity to impressive still-standing Roman buildings like the fortress baths and the central tetrapylon.

Lodge Hill shows that there was other late Romano-British activity nearby. We excavated sherds of third and fourth-century pottery, some late fourth century, showing that after the army left someone was back in the hill fort. That struck some people as very exciting. In more modern times, Lodge Hill has attracted a number of mythic tales and mysterious explanations. In fairness, the earliest written description and plan, provided by William Coxe in his 1801 *An Historical Tour of Monmouthshire*, characterised the site quite accurately. He noted that Bellingstoke, as the site was sometimes called, 'bears more the appearance of a British, than of a Roman encampment'. Given the long-standing 'Arthurian associations' attributed to Caerleon, however, later observers made grander claims. What better location for Camelot!

CAERMELOT

Channel 4 UK's *Time Team* crew thought the Camelot idea was sufficiently entertaining to pursue. They were filming for an Arthurian special and were delighted to find a team working on a reoccupied hill fort, particularly one overlooking Caerleon. When Dr Josh Pollard and I were interviewed on site for the programme, it didn't take long for the 'A word' to come up. 'Tell me, archaeologically, how do you demonstrate Arthur?' we were asked. We looked at one another and responded, 'Don't think you can do'.

There was an immediate call of 'Cut!'. It was then put to us that there really must be a way and that providing one for the viewers would make 'good television'. Despite such urging, we couldn't think of a persuasive way to provide a 'definitive' answer and decided that it was best to leave it there and carry on with the excavation. Later that day, after the film crews had gone, over a cup of tea we kicked ourselves. We suddenly thought what we should have said – 'well, a sword in a stone would help'. What an opportunity missed!

The Roman legions return to Caerleon

In seriousness, the fascination with Arthur is both interesting and important. Myths often drive history and Geoffrey of Monmouth's imaginative 12th-century 'history' not only launched Arthur as a hugely popular theme in the later Middle Ages but also placed Caerleon at the heart of the tales. It is not surprising that Lodge Hill was also incorporated into the Arthurian legend.

In point of fact, the late Roman/early medieval significance of the site may be more prosaic but no less important. The Royal Commission has suggested that hill fort reoccupation, which occurred widely, may have been in large part because such sites 'retained some legal importance in connection with land tenure'. This is an attractive explanation which may explain the reoccupation of many hill forts in Wales and beyond. A folk memory of authority over land exercised from the hill forts would go a long way toward explaining their reoccupation. A good case can be made that Lodge Hill was especially important in this respect. When the army established itself in Caerleon, it carved out a huge *territorium*, land exploited directly to support the troops, in the Usk Valley. When the army departed, control over the *territorium* would presumably have gone as well and this fertile land must have been very attractive. Lodge Hill, with its pre-conquest associations, may have been seen as the most effective way to stake a claim.

SYMBOLS OF AN ANCIENT PAST

In this retention of importance, the hill forts became more than remnants of the past. They, and those who occupied them, became stake holders in a developing present. Symbols of an ancient past retained real relevance to later generations.

There are few places where changing views of a mythic past shaping later Welsh history can be seen more clearly than in Caerleon. Standing Roman monumental structures like the fortress bath and the tetrapylon at the centre of the fortress survived well into the later Middle Ages by which time they had taken on meanings very different from those ascribed to them by the Romans. Both these buildings stood through the 12th century only to be demolished in the early decades of the 13th, probably on the orders of the Anglo-Norman marcher lord William Marshal. It seems that they were pulled down because they had become too closely associated with a period of Welsh revival which threatened the Anglo-Norman ascendancy.

Similarly, Geoffrey's Arthurian tales caused other Roman survivals to take on new meaning. In 1405 armies of Owain Glyndŵr and his French allies were

Human diggers in pursuit of the Romans near Lodge Hill

reported to have camped at the site of Arthur's Round Table in Caerleon. The decayed Roman amphitheatre had been appropriated into the Arthurian tradition!

At Lodge Hill, memories of the intensity of the Silurian War encouraged Roman troops to slight the defences. At the end of the Roman period, the lingering but still potent tradition of the hill fort as a symbol of land tenure encouraged people to occupy it again. In due course, it would gain Arthurian connotations of its own. For all these reasons, Lodge Hill justifies its inclusion in this compilation of the important, sometimes mythic, buildings and places in Welsh history.

Lodge Hill still looms large over Caerleon, in more ways than one. It gives us a direct link to our Celtic ancestors, physical evidence of the Roman conquest, important insights into the early medieval transition, and an ever-changing mythic tradition which can still excite modern film crews and local residents alike. A hill fort is an obvious choice for our favourite historical building as it takes us back to our ancient roots. Lodge Hill is one of our best examples of these iconic structures and I am very happy to make it my choice.

Further reading:
J. Pollard, R. Howell, A. Chadwick and A. Leaver, *Lodge Hill Camp, Caerleon and the Hill forts of Gwent*, BAR British Series 407 (2006)

3

LITTLE AND LARGE – LLYN FAWR AND LLYN CERRIG BACH

Raimund Karl

Today, Llyn Fawr in the Cynon valley and Llyn Cerrig Bach on Anglesey are two entirely unremarkable ponds. In the first millennium BC, however, they seem to have been anything but unremarkable. It can be argued that they are two of the most important places for Welsh (pre-) history.

While certainly significant places in parts of the first millennium BC, this does not mean that they were particularly outstanding even in their heyday. It is indeed very likely that back then, there were many other sites quite like them, some of which may well have been much more important than the two selected here. However, we know nothing of these other sites, since they have not survived into the present, or at least as yet have not been discovered. Thus Llyn Fawr and Llyn Cerrig Bach are as important as representatives of a category of places as they are their own right.

What connects Llyn Fawr and Llyn Cerrig Bach, located far apart in the south and north of the country, is the way they were used by later prehistoric populations. They were used to deposit objects permanently, out of the reach of human hands, presumably as offerings to the gods. And not just any objects. Rather, the objects were seemingly carefully selected because they were valuable, or demonstrated power, or status, and wealth.

LLYN FAWR AND 'HALLSTATT' EUROPE

Llyn Fawr is located in the upper Cynon valley. Originally smaller than today, it was expanded and converted into a reservoir in the early years of the 20th century. It was during these works that the Llyn Fawr hoard was found. The hoard has given its name to the transition phase between the latest Bronze

Age and the early Iron Age, dated to roughly the eighth century BC, because it contains some of the earliest iron objects to be discovered in Britain.

Yet, it also represents the culmination of a practice that became increasingly important during the late Bronze Age (which in Wales started, roughly, in the 12th century BC): the deposition of metalwork, particularly in lakes and other watery places. And it is both this practice, as well as some of the finds made in the lake, that connect Wales with a much wider world, because depositing wealth, particularly high-status metal objects, is a phenomenon that can be observed across wide areas of late Bronze Age and Iron Age Europe: the ancient 'Celtic world'.

The Llyn Fawr hoard itself consists of a mix of different items. Some of them, particularly remains of an iron sword, are heralding the adoption of the new metal which defined the following age. These were exciting new things, only having come into circulation quite recently at the time they were deposited. Others, like two bronze cauldrons, were certainly old already when they were deposited in the lake, and of a type that had a long history, having been in circulation as early as the 11th century BC, perhaps even somewhat earlier than that.

A handful of the many treasures found in Llyn Cerrig Bach

But whether fancy new sword or cherished old cauldron, the objects themselves point at increasingly wide-ranging links that the prehistoric Welsh had established during the previous centuries; links with the so-called 'Hallstatt' cultures on the European continent.

The bronze cauldrons were made from riveted bronze sheet metal, a technique requiring exceptional skills in bronze working. The earliest types of vessels created in this technology had been developed in far distant central Europe by bronze smiths living in the Hungarian plains and Transylvania. But while the earliest example of these types of vessels known from Wales, the Arthog bucket, is thought to be an imported piece, the cauldrons in the Llyn Fawr hoard were made somewhere in Britain, perhaps even quite locally. Clearly associated with feasting, these cauldrons reference a culture of hospitality and gift-exchange between late Bronze Age elites on a previously unprecedented scale.

The iron sword also shows 'continental' links. First of all, the very fact that it is one of the earliest Iron finds in Britain, with the technology of iron working adopted from the continent, constitutes such a connection. Moreover, the sword itself is of a type called *Gündlingen*, after a German find; the sword type that marks the Bronze to Iron Age transition: about half of the known Gündlingen swords were still cast in bronze, while the other half were made from iron.

A UNIQUE WEAPON

Making swords from iron at this time was so new that not even the continental metalworkers had fully understood ironworking: the design of this sword type is suited much more to casting in bronze than iron smithing. In Britain, the Llyn Fawr sword is unique in this respect: it is the only iron Gündlingen type sword known from these islands, though there are many bronze ones known. Rather, the next known iron examples of Gündlingen swords come from central France, with their distribution centre found in southern Germany.

Yet, there is little reason to believe that the iron sword from Llyn Fawr was an imported piece. After all, there are two other iron objects in the hoard, a spear and a socketed sickle, which seem to be local products. Iron smithing was being adopted locally, and thus, the sword could equally well have been made locally. Again, the hoard shows that complex cutting-edge metalworking technologies had been adopted and were being adapted locally.

LLYN CERRIG BACH AND 'LA TÈNE' EUROPE

Llyn Cerrig Bach is located on Anglesey, just beyond the end of the runway at RAF Valley airbase. In fact, the finds here were made when peat was extracted from the boggy shores of Llyn Cerrig Bach to prepare the landing ground for the airbase in 1942. In what is perhaps the most remarkable element of the story of its discovery, an iron chain discovered during the peat extraction works was used and found to be useful for dragging lorries that had got stuck onto firm ground with a tractor. This chain, under later examination, turned out to be a late Iron Age slave gang-chain. While today Llyn Cerrig Bach is a small lake, in the late Iron Age, it may very well have been a tidal inlet.

Llyn Cerrig Bach stands in the same tradition of depositing high-status objects in watery contexts as the Llyn Fawr hoard, though this practice had become somewhat less prevalent during the time that had passed since the depositions at Llyn Fawr. Dating roughly from the period between the second century BC and the first century AD, the finds at Llyn Cerrig Bach come from the very end of the Iron Age. Depositions may well have been ongoing throughout this period, and there is a distinct possibility that deposition at this spot came to an end during the Roman conquest of Ynys Môn. Again, it is the depositional practices, as well as the objects, that link this site with wider 'Celtic' Europe.

Much like the Llyn Fawr hoard, the Llyn Cerrig Bach assemblage is a sizeable number of objects (144 preserved objects or fragments of objects), though due to the method of its discovery, it is likely that many more were lost. Most of these items can be assigned to a social elite: there are numerous swords, some still in ornately decorated scabbards, spears, decorated shield bosses, parts of chariots, cauldrons, and of course that slave gang-chain. And also, once again, there are sickles. Many of the objects also are conspicuously decorated in the art style characteristic of much of the later European Iron Age, the so-called La Tène style. Thus, the objects found at Llyn Cerrig Bach, particularly through their decoration, link North Wales with a wider European information exchange network in which complex methods of constructing art and decorative motives seem to have flowed freely over long distances.

Along with the art style, it is also the selection of objects, and the way of depositing them at Llyn Cerrig Bach that links this particular site with many similar sites on the continent, not least with La Tène itself.

Equally significantly, similar selections of objects are also known from other depositions in continental Europe, most importantly the so-called 'Gaulish sanctuaries'. These sites are mostly known from North-Western France, though similar examples have more recently been discovered as far East as Austria. Characterised by square enclosures and, frequently,

LA TÈNE

La Tène, which gave its name to this art style, is a site in Switzerland, at the shores of – and in – Lake Neuchâtel. Discovered in 1857, when water levels were particularly low, numerous finds were first dredged and, in later decades, excavated, from the lake bed and lake shore: mostly weapons and other high-status equipment, mostly dating to the third and early second century, but continuing also into the first century BC. Again, there are numerous swords, often still in scabbards, spearheads, shields, but also parts of chariots, cauldrons, and even sickles. Similar depositions have since become known from several other Swiss river and lakeshore sites, including Bern Tiefenau, Port Nidau, and Corneaux.

evidence for rather peculiar practices of treating dead human bodies, these sites have often and quite directly been associated with the druids, mentioned in sources from classical antiquity; and also later on in medieval Irish and Welsh literature. Again, depositions of high-status objects abound at these sites, with weapons, chariot parts and similar items found in large numbers.

DEPOSITIONS, DRUIDS, AND HIGHER EDUCATION IN WALES

Depositions like the ones found in Llyn Fawr and Llyn Cerrig Bach can thus, quite clearly, be interpreted in a very specific spiritual context – that of the druids and ancient Celtic religion – which in itself makes them very important sites in Welsh History.

Though not writing about Wales, classical authors like Strabo report that 'the Celts' offered up wealth to the gods, not least by depositing it in lakes. Quite frequently, this may have been spoils of war, including, perhaps, the remains of some of the vanquished, as may be evident in the 'Gaulish sanctuaries'. And writing about Wales, and Anglesey in AD61 specifically, Tacitus in his Annals reports of Suetonius Paulinus conquering Anglesey and destroying the 'groves consecrated to their [the druids'] savage cults' – the time when, roughly, deposition of artefacts at Llyn Cerrig Bach seems to have ended.

Of course, the link between the druids and Llyn Fawr is much more tenuous; after all, there are about seven hundred years between the depositions at Llyn Fawr and the first historical reports about British druids. Yet, the similarities in the depositional practices make it likely that a group of religious practitioners with beliefs not all too unlike those of the much later attested druids was responsible for the creation of the Llyn Fawr hoard.

But there is even more to the lakes than that. Through their link with the druids, and also their exceptional finds, the two sites also provide us with the first evidence for higher education in Wales.

Caesar, in his commentaries on the Gaulish Wars, writes an excursus about the Gauls. In this excursus, he devotes some paragraphs to the druids and their education. He writes that to become a druid, a student would have had to learn a great many verses, so that some would remain twenty years in training. According to Caesar and other classical authors, the druids were theologians and philosophers, historians, mathematicians and scientists, healers and physicians, and also trained in law. In other words, the druids are the graduates of the European Iron Age, those who went through higher education and trained in highly specialised academic skills. And it was Caesar who informed us that druidism had started in Britain, and only later been transferred to the Continent. And he also reported that those Gauls who would study it most diligently, as a rule, would journey to Britain to learn it.

But where would these foreign students learn druidism, if not in the sacred groves of British druids like those at Llyn Fawr and Llyn Cerrig Bach? Thus, those two seemingly unremarkable ponds are probably part of the first higher education institutions we can find in Wales, which make them even more significant in Welsh history.

But the objects found at these locations also tell us about education in craft and industry. The bronze cauldrons and the iron sword in the Llyn Fawr

The 'unremarkable pond' of Llyn Cerrig Bach

hoard, and much of the La Tène artwork in the Llyn Cerrig Bach hoard, tell us about technological information that spread very quickly, and was picked up and developed equally quickly, by local craftsmen and artists. But the highly specialised skills required for much of these works could not simply be picked up by word of mouth, or by looking at the finished object. Rather, these also needed to be taught and learned, perhaps in some early form of apprenticeships. And the fact that several of the techniques and skills seem to have been picked up very quickly, shortly after they had been developed in places as far away as east Central Europe, tells us that the later prehistoric Welsh craftsmen were also exceptionally well connected. Whether they went abroad to learn their craft, or at least train in new skills, or learnt from those craftsmen who came to Britain, perhaps to train as druids, is of course unknown.

Llyn Fawr and Llyn Cerrig Bach thus are extremely important places in Welsh History. They are places that show us how well, and how widely, the later prehistoric Welsh were already connected. They also show us that keeping at the cutting edge of technological and intellectual development is dependent on having a good higher education system, and on the free flow of ideas, both into and out of the country.

4

THE WELSHMAN, THE IRISHMAN AND THE VIKING – ABERLLEINIOG CASTLE

Dave Wyatt

A FORGOTTEN CASTLE WITH A HIDDEN HISTORY

Most people in Wales are aware of the mighty ring of Edwardian castles in the north of the country built in the wake of Edward I's conquest in the late 13th century. Edward's 'iron ring' of fortifications were designed to be symbols of his power and domination over the previously independent Welsh kingdom of Gwynedd. Yet fewer people are aware of another much earlier attempt to subdue Gwynedd through the construction of a network of castles in the years that followed the Norman Conquest. Aberlleiniog Castle, which nestles in a beautiful location near the village of Llangoed close to the eastern shores of Anglesey, lies at the very heart of this hidden history.

Situated just a few miles from Beaumaris's huge Edwardian fortification, Aberlleiniog Castle is a simple yet well preserved Norman motte and bailey fortress, built on the orders of Hugh d'Avranches, Earl of Chester, one of the first marcher lords appointed by William the Conqueror to the Welsh frontier. Today, the motte at Aberlleiniog is crowned by a much later structure, probably a civil war fort, which appears to date to the middle of the 17th century. Yet it is arguably the early medieval history of this site which bears witness to one of the most significant yet little known conflicts in medieval Welsh history: the battle of Anglesey Sound in 1098. This battle reconfigured the geo-political map of North Wales and reversed ambitions of conquest from the east for almost two hundred years, allowing an independent and vibrant Welsh dynasty to flourish in Gwynedd.

ANGLESEY, WALES, AND THE VIKING WORLD

We are often presented with an Anglocentric view of Welsh history with relationships between Wales and England taking centre stage. Yet, it is important to remember that Wales is a westward facing peninsula with a mountainous interior which, to this day, hampers communications between both the north and south and the east and west. In the early middle ages, these internal topographical barriers would have been compounded further by widespread forestation and political fragmentation. Wales, at this time, was made up of a patchwork of competing native kingdoms vying for power and territory. The one unifying topographical feature in Wales was the sea and many of the early medieval Welsh kingdoms had important westward maritime contacts and interactions, both peaceful and violent, with Ireland and the wider Viking world.

The Vikings first came to the Irish Sea region in small sea-borne raiding bands at the end of the eighth century. Over the course of the ninth and tenth centuries they established significant power bases and settled in locations across the Irish Sea region: in the Northern and Western Isles of Scotland, the Isle of Man, Galloway, Cumbria and coastal areas of Ireland. These Viking settlers soon became embroiled in local politics, formed alliances, intermarried and many adopted Christianity, yet they retained a distinct identity signalled through their material culture, language and their warrior outlook. By the middle of the tenth century they had also established vibrant and bustling urban ports such as Dublin, at which mercenaries could be hired and where goods could be exchanged and redistributed across the Viking world. Unsurprisingly, the mastery of maritime routes in the region was very important for the Irish Sea Vikings. Perhaps the most important of these routes was the seaway linking Dublin with a significant Viking settlement in the Wirral which, in turn, connected overland to the Viking city of York. This busy Viking route meant that the island of Anglesey and the coasts of North Wales were of immense strategic significance.

Given all this, it would be very surprising if there had then been no such Viking settlement within Wales. Evidence from native Welsh sources does suggest that Viking forces over-wintered in parts of Wales. There is also a general tradition of Viking settlement in the region in the later Old Norse saga literature. Furthermore, the prevalence of Scandinavian place-name elements for coastal features in Wales is also suggestive of close contact and possible Viking settlement.

THE ISLAND OF THE ENGLISH!

Names with 'ey' endings denote an islet or island in the Old Norse language, for example Bardsey and even Anglesey, which literally means the Island of the English! Coastal names with such Viking elements occur right around Wales and certainly reflect the maritime dominance of the Vikings in the Irish Sea region. However, it must be noted that many of these coastal features retained their Welsh names such as *Ynys Môn* (Anglesey) so it is problematic to argue that they are necessarily indicative of settlement.

In addition to the historical and place-name evidence there is also significant archaeological evidence for Viking activity, especially along the coasts of North Wales and Anglesey. Hoards of buried booty at sites like Orme's Head, Viking burials at Benllech and Viking art styles on the stone cross at Penmon are suggestive of both cultural interaction and Viking settlement. In the last twenty years, a significant defended Viking trading-settlement has also been uncovered at Llanbedrgoch near Red Wharf Bay close to Aberlleiniog castle.

Aberffraw, the medieval seat of the kingdom of Gwynedd

This settlement contained high status Viking artefacts such as merchant's weights, ringed pins, buckles, a whetstone for sharpening swords, Viking style long houses and even non-Christian burials. The site's location and tenth century date appear to have significant implications. Indeed, why would a native Welsh ruler of Gwynedd, whose traditional court was at Aberffraw, just 16 miles away, allow such a high status defended Viking site to exist so close to their seat of power? Does Llanbedrgoch indicate a possible Viking takeover of Anglesey?

GRUFFUDD AP CYNAN – VIKING OR WELSHMAN?

The intimate contacts between Aberlleiniog, Anglesey and the Viking World are further highlighted by the career of one of Gwynedd's most significant medieval kings, Gruffudd ap Cynan (1055–1137). Gruffudd established a powerful independent Welsh dynasty which dominated Gwynedd's political scene over the course of the 12th century. Yet, despite these credentials Gruffudd was in fact only half Welsh. When his grandfather, Iago ab Idwal (king of Gwynedd 1023–1039), was slain in a dynastic dispute, his father, Cynan, fled to Viking Dublin. Dublin was a popular haven for political refugees

Aerial view of the Viking Island of the Bards

from Wales in the 11th century. The ruling Scandinavian dynasty there, the Silkenbeards, were also very interested in maintaining strategic control over the sea routes and raiding interests in North Wales. Unsurprisingly then, an alliance was soon established between Cynan, the disaffected heir to the throne of Gwynedd, and Rhanillt, a daughter of the Silkenbeard dynasty. Gruffudd ap Cynan was a product of this inter-ethnic union and was raised in the Irish Viking settlement of Swords. During his childhood his Viking kin would have been well aware of his potential as a member of one of the leading families of Dublin with a claim to the throne of Gwynedd. It is unsurprising then, that when Gruffudd eventually returned to claim his patrimony in Wales in 1075, that Anglesey was his first target.

Gruffudd ap Cynan is unique in that he is the only 11th-century Welsh king to be the subject of a medieval biography, *The History of Gruffudd ap Cynan* (*HGC*). The historical details within this text are not wholly reliable but it does contain much that can be corroborated by other contemporary sources. It gives us an especially interesting window on Gruffudd's early career. The *HGC* suggests that as Gruffudd strove to regain the throne of Gwynedd he consistently targeted Anglesey and employed military backing from his Viking supporters in Ireland. Indeed, the *HGC* suggests that his own personal bodyguard consisted of Viking warriors who, at times, proved unruly and unpopular with his native Welsh subjects. The *HGC* also suggests that Gruffudd deliberately targeted the recently established Norman castles in Gwynedd. For example, it tells us that in 1075 Gruffudd secured a tenuous control over Anglesey and then attacked the Norman stronghold at Degannwy where he fought with the Norman baron Robert of Rhuddlan and 'other fierce knights of the French'. Gruffudd's strategy in this respect does not appear to have endeared him to the newly settled Normans and in the 1080s he was captured and imprisoned at Chester for over a decade. He managed to escape and in 1094 appears to have resumed his campaign. The *HGC* reveals that at around this time Gruffudd besieged the Norman Castles at Nefyn, on the Llŷn peninsula, and Aberlleniog, on Anglesey again with the support of a Viking fleet, this time from the Isle of Man.

THE NORMANS IN NORTH WALES

It is perhaps important to say a little about the 11th-century Norman activities in Wales at this juncture. Following his victory at Hastings, William the Conqueror established a series of buffer territories or marcher earldoms on the borders of Wales and placed them under the control of tough and trusted Norman leaders. He gave these leaders wideranging powers which appear to have included a licence to launch individual campaigns against the Welsh kingdoms. Attack being the best form of defence, William's marcher earls proceeded to carve out lordships and built castles at key locations to secure their new territories. These early Norman fortifications in Gwynedd were of a type that may have originally been designed in the low-lying coastal areas of northern France which were also vulnerable to coastal attacks from the Vikings. They consisted of a motte or enditched mound which supported a wooden strongpoint overshadowing an enclosed courtyard or bailey. Aberlleiniog is a classic example of such a castle.

Across the Straits – Anglesey and the mainland

In North Wales, a castle building initiative of this kind was undertaken by Hugh d'Avranches, Earl of Chester, and his warlike vassal Robert of Rhuddlan. During the final quarter of the 11th century Hugh and Robert extended their military expansion deep into Gwynedd's heartlands, establishing a line of castles at strategic locations along the North Wales coast which stretched from Flintshire in the east to Llŷn in the West. Aberlleiniog was clearly a crucial link in this chain of coastal castles which all had commanding outlooks to the sea and appeared to have been positioned primarily for defence against sea-borne attacks. As such, they posed a direct threat to Viking coastal shipping and raiding enterprises.

Soon after Gruffudd's attack on Aberlleiniog, Hugh d'Avranches and another powerful Norman marcher earl, Hugh of Shrewsbury, invaded Gwynedd with a very substantial army. This military surge was presumably intended to quell Gruffudd's insurgency and re-establish Norman rule. In the face of overwhelming Norman forces, Gruffudd retreated to Anglesey and from there across the sea to exile in Ireland. This might very well have been the end of his story and could have heralded the beginning of a Norman rule over Gwynedd which would have negated the later Edwardian Conquest of the 13th century. However, the powerful and longstanding Viking geo-political interests in the region were to put paid to both Norman objectives and to Aberlleiniog castle.

ABERLLEINIOG AND THE BATTLE FOR ANGLESEY SOUND OF 1098

The Welsh, Normans and Dublin-Vikings were not the only political players in the Irish Sea region at this time. Indeed, interest in control over the lucrative trading and raiding networks of the Irish Sea region placed North Wales in an international Viking context, attracting the attention of the powerful Norwegian monarch Magnus Barelegs.

Magnus succeeded to the throne of Norway upon the death of his father, Olaf, in 1093. Olaf's had been a relatively prosperous reign during which Norway had experienced a period of increasing wealth. Much of this wealth was derived from trade with the Irish Sea region and its important markets, including Dublin. Upon his accession to the Norwegian throne Magnus appears to have set his sights on the establishment of a maritime empire which controlled these lucrative sea routes. In 1098 he sailed westwards with a large fleet and took control of the strategically crucial Orkneys. He then moved on the Inner and Outer Hebrides before sailing south taking control of the Isle of Man and the coastal region of Galloway. From studying this progress it seems clear that Anglesey fitted perfectly into his plans for maritime domination of the Irish Sea region.

As already noted, the Norman earls of Chester and Shrewsbury had invaded Gwynedd in 1098 forcing Gruffudd ap Cynan to flee to Ireland at precisely the same time that Magnus's great fleet was prowling the Irish Sea. The Norman army then ravaged Anglesey and set up camp at Aberlleiniog castle close to the shores of Anglesey Sound. The *HGC* notes at this point that Magnus Barelegs's fleet launched a surprise attack on the Norman forces. In the ensuing battle, Magnus himself was said to have killed Earl Hugh of Shrewsbury with an arrow. Following this lightning attack, Magnus's fleet then withdrew leaving the Norman army still on Anglesey. However, they very swiftly retreated all the way back to Chester and made no further attempts to subdue North Wales.

Many historians have viewed the battle for Anglesey Sound as an unplanned and coincidental encounter motivated by the Vikings' swashbuckling spirit. Yet, it seems likely that Magnus Barelegs was mindful of the threat which Norman control over North Wales was posing to Viking raiding and trading activities. The native Welsh chronicler of the princes was very clear concerning Magnus's intentions towards Anglesey stating that he hoped 'to take possession of the countries of the Welsh' and had attacked the Normans because of their 'frequent designs... to devastate the whole country'. So the Welsh chronicler was under no illusion that Magnus knew what the Normans were up to on Anglesey and launched a premeditated lightning attack to halt their advance. Magnus seems to have understood that the Normans had grossly overstretched their lines of communication in Gwynedd. A fact borne out by events as Hugh d'Avranches withdrew his forces, not just from Anglesey, but from most of Gwynedd. The battle at Aberlleiniog had therefore highlighted the vulnerability of the Normans' position in North Wales. Their coastal bases were exposed to Viking maritime raids as well as native Welsh attacks from the interior. The Battle of Anglesey Sound marked a significant turning point in the Norman strategy towards Gwynedd whereby attempts at military conquest were abandoned in favour of diplomatic relations.

Following the Battle of Anglesey Sound, Magnus appears to have allowed Gruffudd ap Cynan to return as a client ruler. The Welsh Chronicler tells us that Magnus appeared on Anglesey again in 1102 cutting down timber for his fortresses on Man. That he was able to do so unhindered suggests that Gruffudd ap Cynan at least felt indebted to him. In reality, Gruffudd probably had little option but to comply – the King of Norway, not England, seems have been the real power with whom the Welsh had to contend with in the early 12th century.

As for Aberlleiniog Castle? Well it seems to have been abandoned and quickly fallen into disrepair as did the memory of the significant battle of 1098 which remains uncelebrated. Yet, arguably Aberlleiniog bore witness to one of the most pivotal moments in medieval Welsh history. Had the Normans managed to establish themselves in the North, then an independent and vibrant native Welsh kingdom of Gwynedd could never have flourished. Welsh history, language and culture would undoubtedly have been very different without the Vikings of the Irish Sea.

Further reading:
Davies, Wendy (ed.) *From the Vikings to the Normans* (2003)

5

AN AURA OF *HIRAETH* – STRATA FLORIDA

David Austin

WHERE IS IT AND WHAT IS THERE?

Strata Florida is the site of a former Cistercian Abbey which, in its heyday in the 13th and 14th centuries, loomed large in the culture and politics of Wales and even now wears an aura of *hiraeth* as an icon of Welsh historical identity. It lies in a beautiful little valley just nudged into the western flank of the Cambrian Mountains, on the western, Ceredigion, side. Through the valley flow the clear waters of Afon Teifi along a broad-bottomed glaciated floor, just a mile from its source in Teifi Pools. To put the monastery where its ruins are today, the monk designers and engineers had to manage these waters with their capacity to flood and form marshes. They even diverted its tributary, Afon Glasffrwd, into a hand-dug canal, retaining its course behind a robust stone wall which can still be seen today if you know where to look. Even today the valley rarely floods and on this island of freshly drained land the monastery was laid out and built from 1184 onwards.

The remains of the Abbey, closed in 1539 by Henry VIII's Dissolution of the Monasteries, have never been entirely lost to view, but very quickly its lead roof was stripped off and the walls became a quarry for local buildings. This asset stripping very soon left little to see in the way of architecture and it is clearly no Tintern or Valle Crucis. One piece of architecture did survive, however, and this in itself is a curiosity given the fate of the rest. The west front of the Abbey church, through which Huw Edwards walked in episode two of the BBC's *Story of Wales*, is still there: it is the one place in the whole structure where Celtic art was used, set around the arch of its unique great doorway.

This use of a stylistic tradition stretching back into the Bronze Age was clearly intended to have allusion to a deep ancestral past, and its position at the point where the great and the good of the world once passed into the sacred spaces of the church is clearly meaningful. What constantly amazes me is that this meaning, never written about in any surviving document, seems to have kept the arch safe as a succession of gentry owners down the centuries protected and restored this one element of the place, as a memorial. It is the architectural jewel of Strata Florida and today fully protected and presented to the public on behalf of the nation by the Welsh Government's heritage organisation, Cadw.

FINDING MORE

Since the late 1990s, along with several of my archaeology and history colleagues at the University of Wales Trinity St David, I have been working on discovering more of what has been lost, and trying to get at the intentions behind the Abbey's creation. Ours, though, was not the first act of revelation and research. It is notable that from its very first years Wales's foremost national society studying the material culture of our country, the Cambrian Archaeological Association (affectionately known as 'the Cambrians' and founded in 1846), focussed on Strata Florida as one of its main sites of interest, visiting it on many occasions over the last 160 or more years. Under its auspices the first holes were dug in the late 1840s to understand the largely

An archaeological treasure

by then earthwork remains. Then in the late 1880s, backed by the Cambrians, railway engineer Stephen Williams set about uncovering the whole of the church and part of the cloister. It is still these foundations and some of his finds which the modern tourist visitor can see today on site and in a recently refurbished exhibition.

However, I am fond of saying that Strata Florida is a place 'with a big history but a small physical presence'. For specialists it has always been clear that the original site must have been much larger than Williams revealed. We know from other, better-preserved sites, like Tintern or Fontenay in the Burgundian heartlands of the Cistercian Order, that there would have been a number of stone buildings ranged around the church within an inner, walled precinct. There would also have been a larger outer precinct containing farm buildings, gardens, orchards and other activities essential to keeping the monastery and its inhabitants running. So, in the Strata Florida Research Project we set about trying to find them and what we have found has astonished us.

The most surprising thing is that our survey, prospecting (geophysics) and trial excavations have led us to believe that the Abbey was originally spread out across much of the valley floor and may have covered as much as 100 to 120 acres. This is still a work in progress, but if we are right, then Strata Florida was laid out to be one of the largest, if not *the* largest, Cistercian Abbey in Britain. We can be quite sure that the inner precinct alone would have swallowed up the whole of the Abbey of Whitland, the monastery in Carmarthenshire from which Strata Florida was originally founded. This precinct has at its heart an enormous open space in front of the west façade of the church. That fabulous door with its Celtic art could be seen across a vast expanse of cobbles by any visitor who came through the great two-storey gatehouse between the inner and outer precincts. This is the building that we have exposed in our current programme of excavations.

Strata Florida (Crown copyright: Royal Commission on Ancient and Historical Monuments, Wales)

This sense of space within the core monastic complex buildings is very unusual. It echoes the large gathering places to be found in front of the main pilgrimage centres of Europe. Yet, although there is an oral tradition of pilgrimage to Strata Florida, there is nothing in the record to suggest that this was something ever sanctioned by the medieval church. There is no known shrine there, unlike at St Davids, a destination celebrated in Welsh history. We do know, however, that pilgrims on their way down to the south-western tip of Wales from the north, as well as other travellers, visited Strata Florida and sought rest and food in one of its two guesthouses. There must have been many: we think we can identify one of these guesthouses in the geophysics, and it is as large as the church.

Although size isn't everything, the scope of Strata Florida's design is remarkable and needs explanation, but already we are clear that it is a significant part of its meaning. Just imagine that, in the later years of the 12th century, in the countryside west of the great wall of the Cambrian mountains, a society which had scarcely seen a stone building, was still largely subsistence farming and not yet engaged in the money economy would see a huge enterprise undertaken at the heart of which was a piece of architecture to rival a small cathedral. It must have been a source of awe. A big European corporation had arrived and set up business. New rites were performed, rivers were diverted, bogs drained, woodland felled, stone brought from Somerset and from the whole of Wales, new industrial technologies introduced, and the monks and their workforce set about transforming the whole landscape and economy of this region forever.

LAND AND LANDSCAPE

The establishment of a big operation like this was not to be undertaken lightly. But there was a formula for success and all was in the name of a life given to God. At the core was the dynamism of an idea, the Cistercian idea. It was fundamentally an adaptation of an older principle created by the Desert Fathers in North Africa and the Holy Land in the fourth and fifth centuries, and then codified into a monastic rule by St Benedict at Monte Cassino in southern Italy in the early sixth century. The Rule established a highly disciplined pattern of life, dedicated to prayer and study and to the hard physical work of providing food, shelter and clothing for the men (and later women) who chose to live together in communities behind the walls of a monastery. The work was indeed seen as part of the act of prayer: the aim to make the desert places fertile as a gift to God.

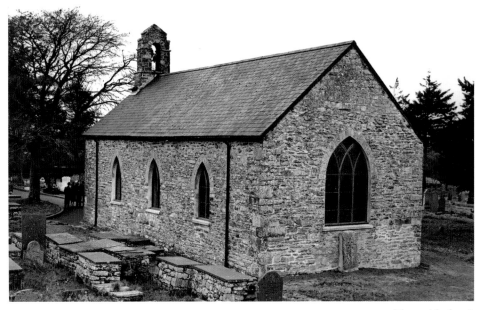

The parish church

By the end of the 11th century there were monasteries all over Europe and in parts of north Africa. Many felt by then, however, that the old principles at the heart of the Rule had been fatally compromised and become corrupt. The source of that corruption was, ironically, the other main component of the monastic formula. Kings, princes and barons of the feudal world got the spiritual and administrative support of the Church if they endowed the monasteries with sufficient land to let them lead the monastic life. The prize for giving this land was the promise of eternal salvation. So successful was this arrangement that some of these monasteries had become very rich. In these circumstances the monasteries became worldly and the standards dropped.

So a few disillusioned Benedictine monks broke away and founded a monastic order which sought to re-establish the original discipline of the Rule. Their first new establishment was at Cîteaux in Burgundy; hence the name Cistercians. This movement created such enthusiasm that within a century over five hundred new monasteries had been created from one end of Europe to the other. The irony was that, again, and very quickly they in turn attracted large grants of land, albeit often wildernesses 'away from the congress of men' among forests, bogs and moorland, as at Strata Florida. The Cistercian work ethic of constant prayer and work, however, also meant that these wildernesses were soon transformed and great revenues were generated leading again to the trap of corrupting wealth.

A RIVAL'S RECOMMENDATION

The rival Benedictine Gerald of Wales, one of the most lively writers of the Welsh middle ages, was no lover of the Cistercians, especially those of Strata Florida whom he accused of stealing his books. Yet he had a sneaking admiration. 'Give them', he wrote, 'a wilderness or a forest, and, in a few years, you will find a dignified Abbey in the midst of smiling plenty'. Of Strata Florida in particular he said: 'it was in the course of time enriched far more abundantly with oxen, studs of horses, herds of cattle and flocks of sheep, and the riches they produced, than all the houses of the same order throughout Wales'. Indeed the land they were given also had a larger footprint of acres than any other contemporary monastery in Wales.

Our research in this landscape has shown us that, indeed, they changed much, especially in the few square miles around the abbey itself. They also introduced advanced techniques of mining and metal processing to exploit the vast mineral wealth of the Cambrian Mountains. Yet they also left much alone, choosing rather to promote the well-being of their tenant farmers by the introduction of new technology like the water-wheel, by the demonstration of new systems of stock and crop management, famously sheep farming on the upland and, most of all, by the connection to the trading networks and money economy of Europe. In this way the wilderness was transformed, but the traditional Welsh pattern of ancient dispersed farms was preserved and enhanced. It is still there today.

PATRONAGE AND THE PURSUIT OF A WELSH IDENTITY

This act of cultural conservation, the large scale of the Abbey and the huge footprint of its lands, the precise use of Celtic art on the western door and the capacity given by its wealth were not accidental. Nor indeed was its promotion of the Welsh native culture and language by the inscription and production of so many of its earliest written texts and by its support of poets and writers. One of these texts was *Brut y Tywysogion* (Chronicle of the Princes), the first history of Wales in Welsh, begun at Llanbadarn Fawr and continued at Strata Florida. One of the great heroes of this account is the Lord Rhys ap Gruffudd, Prince of Deheubarth and Lord of Dinefwr. Although the Abbey was first founded by an Anglo-Welsh knight in 1164, it was really Rhys, by taking Ceredigion back from the Normans in the following year, who was its patron, effectively re-founding it in 1184 and helping the monks to move from its original site at Henfynachlog two miles to the south, to where it is today.

That site, newly drained, however, was not, we think, really new. We are beginning to see evidence that it was built over something earlier. We believe

The past emerges from below

that the Abbey church, the heart of the monastery, was put over the southern edge of an ancient pre-Cistercian burial ground, with its great central crossing embracing a pre-existing holy well. Out of that burial ground, where it had been covered by the new Abbey, stone burial markers were recovered and re-used to mark graves still to be seen in the quiet and protected angle of the crossing tower and presbytery at the east end of the new Abbey Church. These stones were made in the time of the native kings and formed in the same motifs as those of the great west door. Thus in the Abbey church at its west end, the metaphorical place of birth and entry, and at its east end, at the point of death and transcendence, Celtic art is deployed as a marker.

All of this, we feel, was by design; Rhys recruited the Cistercians to the project of creating a great institution in the very heart of Wales. He was well aware of the need, in his modern world of the 12th century, to draw Wales into the family of states then forming within Europe. This would be a source of strength so that Wales might remain independent and resistant to the imperial intentions of neighbours (is this not familiar?). Such institutions were essential to the ambitions of an aspirant state – they guaranteed succession and permanence. Strata Florida, the 'Valley of Flowers', was built, we are sure, for that purpose, at a scale and with a presence to create respect. It is no coincidence that in 1238 Llywelyn Fawr himself came in his old age to Strata Florida, commanding all the native princes under his control to be there and to swear that Dafydd his son would be allowed to assume all of his authority when he died. If that oath had been kept Wales would have been truly founded as a state. Llywelyn was building on Rhys's vision.

In a beautiful, still spiritual, landscape Strata Florida retains all that deep meaning that was embedded within it by design by prince and abbot alike in the 12th and 13th centuries. People who come can feel it. Its poetry drew Dafydd ap Gwilym here. It is indeed a special place in the history of Wales.

Further reading:

Essays by David Austin and Jemma Bezant in Janet Burton and Karen Stöber
 (eds), *Monastic Wales: New Approaches* (2013)

The west front of the abbey church

6

RED DRAGONS, RED BANDITS, RED PRIESTS: THE STRANGE HISTORY OF YSBYTY IFAN

Madeleine Gray

Ysbyty Ifan is a pretty little village in the foothills of Snowdonia, just south of the tourist honeypots of Betws-y-coed. The village sits astride the old border between Denbighshire and Caernarfonshire. The Conwy river is little more than a stream at this point, chattering over its stony bed, but it was once the boundary between the heartland of Gwynedd and the 'Middle Kingdom' of north-east Wales. This was the front line in the final struggle for Welsh independence in the 1280s.

Ysbyty Ifan was the home of the Knights of St John and gave hospitality to both pilgrims and outlaws. Later on, a local family provided some of the foundation stones for modern Wales as we know it. It is at the heart of so much of our history – so why do so few people know where it is?

SAINTS, SOLDIER MONKS AND SANCTUARY THIEVES

The first church in Ysbyty Ifan was built by the Knights of St John, the Knights Hospitallers, who had a hostel there. The Knights of St John were soldier monks, vowed to protect pilgrims on their way to the Holy Land. But they also cared for pilgrims nearer home. Their hostel at Ysbyty Ifan is on the ancient pilgrimage route from Bangor-on-Dee and Holywell in north-east Wales to Bardsey, the island of twenty thousand saints in the far north-west. These were the routes that brought pilgrims to Wales, and that knitted Wales into the world of western Christendom

The bridge at Ysbyty Ifan that sits astride the old border between Denbighshire and Caernarfonshire

Not only pilgrims found hospitality there. The Knights had the privilege of sanctuary, but unfortunately it could be abused. In the 15th century, in the troubled time after the Glyndŵr uprising, Ysbyty Ifan was one of the hideouts of some of Wales's most famous outlaws, the notorious Red Bandits of Dinas Mawddwy.

Writing at the end of the 16th century, Sir John Wynn of Gwydir said Ysbyty Ifan had been 'a receptacle of thieves and murderers'. But a new dawn was breaking for Wales, and the people of Ysbyty Ifan were at the heart of the revolution.

THE RED DRAGON LEADS THE WAY

In the church at Ysbyty Ifan are the tombs of some of the founding fathers and mothers of modern Wales. An elaborately carved cross surrounded by vine leaves and fruit commemorates Marared ferch Hywel, who married Hywel ap Cynwrig of Plas Iolyn, a big house just to the east of the village. His grandfather Cynwrig ap Llywarch is remembered by another slab with a sword and shield.

Marared and Hywel's great-grandson was Rhys ap Maredudd of Foelas, another big house on the outskirts of the village. The Welsh played a big part in the Wars of the Roses, supporting whichever side had Welsh leaders. The Yorkists had land in south-east Wales and Richard III had Welsh royal blood in his veins. But in the summer of 1485, most of Wales supported the Lancastrian Henry Tudor. Rhys ap Maredudd took a local army to meet Henry on his way to challenge Richard III. It was Rhys who rescued Henry's banner of the Red Dragon of Cadwaladr on the battlefield at Bosworth. One Welsh poet even implied that it was Rhys who actually killed Richard III.

Journalistic exaggeration, maybe – and to judge from the skull found at Leicester in 2013, a number of Henry's soldiers could have claimed the fatal blow. But Rhys and his family did well out of the Tudor victory. Their local power and their landed estate grew. Wales did well out of the Tudors, too. Henry never came back to the land of his birth, but he did his best to lift the punishments that had been imposed on the Welsh in reprisal for the Glyndŵr uprising.

With a Welsh king on the throne, Welsh men and women flocked to London in search of fame and fortune. Rhys's son Robert was one of them. He seems to have studied at Oxford but he never finished his degree, though the poets described him as skilled in Hebrew as well as Latin. This might be exaggeration again – but if it was true, it would make Robert one of the leaders of the Renaissance in Wales.

Conwy castle, where the river, which is barely a stream at Ysbyty Ifan, meets the sea

He became Cardinal Wolsey's personal chaplain and cross-bearer. Apparently he was also able to give the great man some valuable legal advice. He never lost his local roots, though. His effigy lies in the church alongside his father's. The effigies have been battered and damaged but they are clearly the memorials of Very Important People.

Rhys is in armour, a sword at his side. His son wears the flowing robes of a priest. By their side is an elegantly-dressed woman. She is usually identified as Rhys's wife, Lowri, but her head-dress is a fashionably French bonnet from the 1520s. Is this really Robert's wife, Mared?

Yes, he was a priest – but yes, like many of the Welsh clergy, he was also married, and he fathered at least 16 children. Two of them became abbots of the Cistercian abbey near Conwy, and founded families of their own. Shock, horror, scandal – or a pragmatic acceptance that a career in the church should not debar you from relationships and family life?

No-one in Wales seems to have been keen on the changes of the Reformation, but clerical families like Robert's would have heard about reformers like Martin Luther and Huldrych Zwingli, who signalled their rejection of Rome by getting married. Religious reform might offer some advantages to Mared and her family at Foelas.

RENEWAL AND REFORMATION

It's also worth remembering that Robert's work for Cardinal Wolsey would have brought him into close contact with the Cardinal's private secretary – none other than Thomas Cromwell, architect of the Acts of Union and the English Reformation. Henry VIII was less emotionally involved with Wales than his father had been, but in the crisis following the break-up of his marriage and the split with the Catholic church, he was acutely aware of the danger of invasion through Wales. After all, this was how his father had gained a kingdom.

Wales was seen as a wild and lawless country, inadequately controlled by the Marcher lords. How true this was, we may never know. But it is certainly true that the Welsh people were struggling under legal disadvantages that amounted to a policy of apartheid in our own country. We were not allowed to live and trade in towns. We could not become magistrates or government officials. We had no parliamentary representation. We were tied to an outdated legal system with no possibility of reform.

By now, Thomas Cromwell had survived Wolsey's fall and was Henry VIII's right-hand man. He took the advice of Welsh people in London – men like

Robert ap Rhys, who told him that what Wales needed was emancipation and union with England. By the time the Act of Union was passed in 1536, Robert had been dead for over two years, but his advice must have helped to shape Cromwell's policies.

We are so used to regarding the Acts of Union as a betrayal of our independence that we forget that they were welcomed with open arms in 16th-century Wales. They were designed to keep Wales loyal. Possibly one of the reasons why the Welsh accepted religious change was that they had so much to lose if the Acts of Union were torn up.

THE RED DOCTOR

If Cromwell worked closely with Robert ap Rhys, he would have known all about the wife and the 16 children back home in Ysbyty Ifan. And he would almost certainly have been introduced to young Ellis, the second son and the brightest. Ellis took his grandfather's name as one of the newfangled English surnames – his father was Robert ap Rhys and Ellis made this into Ellis Price.

Like his father, Ellis went to university – in his case, to Cambridge. Unlike his father, he acquired several degrees, and gained his doctorate in 1534, when he was only 22. He was nicknamed *Y Doctor Coch*, 'the Red Doctor'. It's generally assumed that this was because he was so proud of his doctorate that he wore his red academic gown on every possible occasion. A bit like wearing your favourite team's football shirt in bed, maybe? As we will see, though, there could be another explanation for his nickname.

The following year, Cromwell sent young Ellis as one of his inspectors of monasteries in North Wales. It wasn't a great success. His fellow commissioners found him a bit of a trial. He showed off about his commission in the taverns. According to one of the other commissioners, he took his 'concubine' with him (actually, it could have been his first wife, Catherine Conway of Bodrhyddan). Ironically, one of the things he was supposed to be checking up on was how well the monks were keeping their vows of celibacy.

Again, we have to remember that Cromwell knew Ellis and his family well. Was he sending coded messages to the clergy of North Wales by sending the son of a priest to inspect them? It was at about this time that the clergy of Gwynedd wrote to Cromwell explaining how difficult their lives would be if they were forced to separate from their wives. They would be unable to offer hospitality or help the poor.

Ellis lost his place on the commission but Cromwell clearly still thought the young man had potential. In 1538 he was one of the men entrusted with the sensitive task of dismantling some of Wales's most popular pilgrimage shrines.

Most of us nowadays would sympathise with the medieval peasants in places like Penrhys who saw their beloved statues taken away and their little shrines destroyed. But you also have to see things from the viewpoint of the reformers. When Ellis went to Llandderfel in North Wales, he found over five hundred people gathered there on St Derfel's Day. According to Ellis's account, they believed that the statue (not God, not even the saint) had the power to rescue the damned from hell. Even an orthodox Catholic would have said that was a dangerous misunderstanding.

Ellis dealt with it by the simple method of removing the statue. The parson and parishioners tried to buy him off with £40 (a huge sum in those days – probably equivalent to over £100k in modern money) but he could not be deterred.

Now, you could say that Ellis had an eye to his future employment prospects and thought it was worth passing up on the £40 in order to keep his job. Or you could say that he actually believed in what he was doing. He had studied at Cambridge, which was becoming a bit of a hotbed of radical ideas by the 1530s. Was he a hypocrite, or an over-enthusiastic young man?

The village of Ysbyty Ifan

It's also worth remembering that Ellis's strategy worked. There could have been a local rebellion like the Pilgrimage of Grace – but there wasn't. When it comes to the Reformation, Wales is a bit like Sherlock Holmes's dog in the night. The curious thing about the dog, if you remember, is that it didn't bark – and the reason why it didn't bark (spoiler alert here) is that it recognised a member of the household. There was no real enthusiasm for change in Wales, but there was very little open resistance either. One of the reasons for this is that English reformers like Cromwell chose local men to put their policies into effect – men like Ellis Price.

BANDITS AT BOSWORTH?

Most of what we know about the Bandits comes from the pen of Sir John Wynn of Gwydir. When he said that 'they had to their backstay friends and receptors, all the country of Merioneth and Powysland', it was a clear dig at the Foelas family who controlled Ysbyty Ifan and were the local rivals of the Wynns. It is even possible that the Bandits formed the core of the fighting force which Rhys took to Bosworth. After all, one man's bandit is another man's freedom fighter.

THE RED BANDITS

So where do the Red Bandits come into the story? Ellis was nicknamed the Red Doctor. This may have been because of his red doctoral robes, but there is another possible explanation, and that is that he had red hair. And the Red Bandits were so called because they too had red hair. So Rhys ap Maredudd and the Bandits could have been cousins – or even closer than cousins.

FORGOTTEN FOUNDATION STONES

Ysbyty Ifan and its church contain some of the foundation stones of modern Wales. The church is always open. So why isn't the village a place of modern pilgrimage? Possibly because we have such difficulties in thinking about what happened in Wales in the 16th century. We are now unpicking a lot of that history. We are used to having our own assembly government – indeed, we now talk just about the 'Welsh Government'. Some of us want to go even further. We all find it hard to accept that the Acts of Union were what the people of Wales wanted, bringing an end to centuries of apartheid-style oppression.

And we have such contradictory perspectives on the Reformation. Our chapel traditions make us very critical of the late medieval church, but we also find it difficult to accept that men like Ellis Price had such difficulty in introducing change – and that a reformer like Cromwell might have to choose a rather dubious young man as his agent in North Wales because of his family's connections.

These buildings, these places, are important. They tell us about who we are, and who we were. But sometimes who we were is not what we think we should have been. We can cling to what we think ought to have happened. Sometimes, though, the historian's job is to unpick these assumptions and to find other ways of looking at the past. If we can understand who we were, and why we did those things that seem strange to us now, we will be better equipped to move on.

And according to local tradition, Abraham Lincoln's great-grandmother Elen Morris also came from Ysbyty Ifan.

Perhaps the Americans should come here on pilgrimage as well?

Further reading:

Glanmor Williams, *Recovery, Reorientation and Reformation: Wales,*
   c 1415–1642 (1987)

7

FIGHTING THE GOOD FIGHT – THE CHURCHES OF THE GOWER

Helen J. Nicholson

Imagine the scene: you are standing at the west end of the Gower Peninsula, in the village of Rhossili, looking out at Worm's Head and across the sea. It is a peaceful summer's evening. The sun is setting, its golden rays dancing on the rippling waves. You can hear the sound of children playing on the beach below, and bird song in the churchyard of Rhossili church nearby.

It's a long way from Jerusalem.

Yet eight hundred years ago, this church was owned by a religious-military organization which existed to aid people in Jerusalem. The Knights Hospitaller

Rhossili

collected funds to protect travellers going to Jerusalem. Their armies fought to defend Jerusalem and the territories which western Europeans had conquered in the Holy Land, during the First Crusade (1096–99) and later.

Nine of the parish churches in the Gower area were controlled by the Knights Hospitaller. To look at them, you wouldn't guess that they had any link with Jerusalem. They are fine, stone-built churches, most dating from the 12th to the 14th centuries, although of course over the last eight hundred-odd years a few repairs have been necessary! In the 19th century, some were so thoroughly restored that little remains of the Hospitallers' buildings. But what we see today is generally similar to what was there when the Hospitallers owned them.

Ilston

WHO WERE THE HOSPITALLERS?

The Hospitallers operated a hospital for poor and sick pilgrims in Jerusalem, helped to defend the roads on which pilgrims travelled in the Holy Land and maintained armies to protect the Europeans who had settled there after the First Crusade. In the Gower area they controlled the churches of Ilston, Llanrhidian, Landimore, Loughor, Port Eynon, Penmaen, Penrice, Rhossili, and St Johns Juxta Swansea. The Hospitallers had the right to choose the priest at each of these churches. They also controlled the church property and received various dues from the parishes, as well as owning other land in the Gower, from which they received rent and other payments. Their profits from the Gower parishes could be sent overseas, far away to the other end of Christendom, to be used to support Christians in faraway lands.

HOW DID THE HOSPITALLERS COME TO OWN SO MUCH OF THE GOWER?

The simple answer is that local landowners gave them these churches and lands. They believed that as the Hospitallers were protecting Christians in the East and helping God's work by caring for the poor sick, they could put themselves right with God and win God's favour by helping the Hospitallers. Most of the donors were of Norman descent, such as Robert de la Mare who gave the church of Port Eynon in around 1165, or William de Turberville who gave the churches of Llanrhidian, Landimore and Rhossili. The Turbervilles were an important local family who also supported the Cistercian monks. Then as now, giving generous charitable donations won respect and influence in society. But it wasn't only the Normans who supported the Hospitallers: Einion and his brother Goronwy ap Llywarch gave them twelve acres of land in Swansea.

Some donations may have been prompted by family connections. John de Braose gave the church at Ilston and additional lands. His grandfather William de Braose had been a patron of the Hospitallers. John also supported the Hospitallers' new women's house at Aconbury in Herefordshire, which had been founded by his aunt, Margaret de Lacy. Did his Aunt Margaret prompt John's generosity?

John and Margaret's support for the Hospitallers may also have been encouraged by events in the Middle East. They made their donations as the Fifth Crusade (1218–21) was being planned and set out. For those who could not go in person to support their fellow Christians' attempt to recover Jerusalem, giving land and money to the Hospitallers who worked to help Christians in the East was an alternative. The Hospitallers' sister order, the Templars, also received a single church in the Gower: Llanmadoc. Countess Margaret of Warwick gave them this property in 1156, perhaps reflecting her family's interest in the crusades. When the Templars were dissolved in 1312, the church passed into the Hospitallers' hands.

Llanmadoc

However, there was another reason for giving property in the Gower to the Hospitallers. The security situation in the Gower was precarious. The land was disputed between rival claimants: within families or between Normans and Welsh. One solution in such cases was to give the disputed property to a religious order – such as the Hospitallers. There was also the problem of piracy in the Severn Estuary. In the 12th-century Viking raiders – based in Ireland, the Isle of Man and the Scottish Isles – still ravaged the Irish Sea coasts. Any passing ship could become a raiding vessel; the crew could easily come to shore on Gower's inviting coasts and carry off animals and even humans for ransom or slavery. Lundy Island, far out in the Channel but within easy reach of the Gower by sea, was a pirate lair during the first half of the 13th century.

It is because of such dangers that Llanrhidian church has a tall tower with stairs up to a battlemented roof, which could be used as a look-out and could house a fire beacon to give warning of raids. As Gower churches are built strongly of stone, they could be used as temporary refuges. Of course no church could withstand a long siege by a determined force of raiders, but a stone-built church could give protection for long enough for relief to arrive. Given the constant danger of attack, it was natural for landowners to entrust these churches to a military religious institution, which in theory had the military as well as the spiritual might to hold raiders at bay. In fact, it doesn't seem that the Hospitallers ever armed their tenants in the Gower or hired soldiers to protect them, but their military reputation and spiritual connections with Jerusalem would help to keep casual raiders away.

WHAT DID THE GOWER CONTRIBUTE TO THE CRUSADES?

The Hospitallers would have agreed to look after these church buildings and appoint the priest, but the donors intended that surplus income would help the Hospitallers' work in the East. The problem was that upkeep of the church buildings and support of the priests could absorb all the income from these parishes, and more.

For example, the present-day Rhossili church is not the original building. In 1980 the remains of an older church were found in the Warren, the sand dunes below the village. It appears that the 12th-century church was engulfed by sand in storms in the early 14th century, and that the present church was a replacement building on higher ground, away from the sea. The beautiful Norman doorway in the present-day church probably came from this older church. But who paid for that elegant new 14th-century church? It must have been the Hospitallers, as the church at Rhossili was their responsibility. Yet from the early years of the 14th century the Hospitallers had many other demands on their money. They were trying to rebuild their organisation after their castles and lands in the Middle East had been conquered by the Mamluks of Egypt; they conquered the island of Rhodes and set up a new hospital there; they organised naval operations against the Turks and the Muslims of Egypt. With these enormous expenses to meet, it's astonishing that the Hospitallers rebuilt Rhossili church as they did. No doubt the bishop of St Davids made sure that they met their responsibilities to the parish. But if the Hospitallers had wished they could probably have got away with a much smaller building.

The same appears to have happened at Penmaen, where the earlier church on Penmaen Burrows was buried by sand in the early 14th century, and a new church was built further inland. This church was so heavily rebuilt in the 19th century that it's now hard to know what the Hospitallers' medieval church looked like.

However, we can still see Cheriton church, which the Hospitallers built in the 13th century, or possibly the early 14th. It replaced Landimore church, which William de Turberville had given the Hospitallers. It's possible that the original Landimore church was on a site nearer the sea and the Hospitallers moved the church site inland to escape bad weather and sea raiders. In any

Cheriton

case, Cheriton is a well-proportioned building, with fine stone carving; worthy of the international institution which built it. But the church is surely more impressive than was necessary for the small community which it serves.

The Hospitallers didn't always go to such expense, however. In August 1400, Bishop Guy Mone of St Davids wrote that some time previously he had visited the church of Llanrhidian as part of his routine tour of his diocese, and found that it was in a tumbledown state, very much in need of repair. He had instructed the master of Slebech in Pembrokeshire, who was the Hospitaller official in charge of the order's properties in south-west Wales, to get the church repaired, but the master had not done anything. As a result, for a long time it had been impossible to hold services in the church. So now the bishop was confiscating the rents, tithes and other income of the church and appointing five parishioners to oversee the rebuilding work. The rebuilding was obviously a success, as the nave did not have to be restored again until the 19th century, and the present-day chancel and tower date from the medieval period.

JACKS AND TURKS

By the late 14th century, the Hospitallers in England and Wales had no resources to spare. The Hospitallers were involved in the crusade against the Ottoman Turks in 1396, which ended in disaster for the western Europeans. The English prior, John Raddington, travelled out to the East several times with money and men to assist the Christian cause. As the Turks advanced into Europe and the combined forces of Christendom seemed powerless to stop them, the needs of one small parish in the Gower peninsula were overlooked. The money which would have been used to mend the roof of Llanrhidian church had already gone to pay soldiers to fight the Turks in eastern Europe.

WHAT'S SPECIAL ABOUT THE GOWER CHURCHES?

Nothing about these churches in the Gower obviously suggests any connection with Jerusalem.

Many churches elsewhere in western Europe which belonged to the Hospitallers or the Templars had a circular nave, as a visual aid to remind passers-by of the Church of the Holy Sepulchre in Jerusalem, and the role which the Hospitallers and Templars played in protecting it against the forces of Islam. In England, the Hospitallers' church at Little Maplestead in Essex and their original church at Clerkenwell, north of the city of London, had circular naves.

None of the Gower churches had circular naves, however, even though the Hospitallers controlled these churches at the time that they were built. There was a church at Ilston before the Hospitallers – reputedly, the ancient yew tree at

Llanrhidian

the church door also predates the Hospitallers – but the current nave was built after the Hospitallers took over. Llanmadoc also existed before it was given to the Templars. The design of the church predates the period when the Templars owned it, but neither they nor the Hospitallers changed the plan to reflect their Jerusalem connections. The same was the case at Llanrhidian, Penmaen and Rhossili. The Hospitallers do not appear to have done any rebuilding at Port Eynon. Their churches at Loughor and in Swansea no longer exist, but there is no evidence that they were circular. Cheriton is designed like a small cathedral with the tower placed between the chancel (where the altar stands) and the nave (where the congregation stood). Clearly the Hospitallers did not skimp on the building, but they didn't include any references to Jerusalem in the plan. Penrice forms the shape of a cross: the nave may predate the Hospitallers, but the north and south transepts – which stick out like the arms of a cross – date from the time that the Hospitallers held the church. Perhaps the Hospitallers deliberately gave the building this symbolic design, but in that case, why did they redesign only one of their churches like this?

How else could the Hospitallers have left their mark here? They could have built a fine house as an administrative base, but they did not. Again, they

Llanrhidian's tower

could have left their mark on the saints to which their churches were dedicated. We might expect them to have abolished the dedications to local saints, rededicating their churches to saints connected to the Holy Land, or at least to their own familiar Norman saints. But here again, just as in church design, the Hospitallers respected local tradition. Cheriton is dedicated to St Cadoc, Ilston and Llanrhidian to St Illtyd, Llanmadoc to St Madoc, Port Eynon to St Cattwg. Rhossili is dedicated to the Blessed Virgin Mary, the most popular dedication both within and outside Wales. Only two of the Hospitallers' churches in the Gower have non-Welsh dedications: Penmaen is dedicated to St John the Baptist, the Hospitallers' own patron saint, and Penrice to St Andrew.

Although nothing about these churches was special to the Hospitallers, the Gower churches are particularly fine buildings. They are well designed, each one individual and unique, but all reflecting the care of architects and builders who took a pride in the work. Despite their international connections, the Hospitallers would not have brought architects and builders in from overseas. They would have used men and supplies from these islands. Yet they had the resources to command good design, workmanship and materials. Perhaps the wealthy men and women who gave the Hospitallers their lands and churches here hoped that the Hospitallers would put much-needed resources into the Gower and boost the economy of the area. If so, they achieved what they hoped for.

CONCLUSION

Most of us now think of the Gower Peninsula as a picturesque and peaceful rural retreat. Rhossili, Llanrhidian, Cheriton and the other Hospitaller churches here are a long way from Jerusalem, but in the middle ages they were part of an international organisation that supported travellers to Jerusalem and fought to maintain a European foothold in the Middle East. Their form reflects the dangers which threatened this now-tranquil area long ago: piracy from the sea, raiders and warfare inland. Despite the ravages of time and restoration these buildings survive to remind us of a turbulent past.

Further Reading
Geoffrey R. Orrin, *The Gower Churches* (1979)

8

NEAREST TO GOD – LLANGWM UCHAF

Alun Withey

A place doesn't necessarily have to be prominent to be important. Often, history teaches us that it is worthwhile to turn our attention towards somewhere perhaps less well known – even anonymous. By focussing on a relatively remote Welsh village in the mid 17th century, I want to show how much we can learn about the daily lives of our forebears, their beliefs, fears, cares and concerns.

In 1671, the people of the small Monmouthshire village of Llangwm Uchaf were involved in a dispute which threatened to divide their normally close community. The village was ablaze with 'divers[e] variances, quarrels and debates' even lawsuits, to 'the utter destruction and overthrow of manie'. What had inflamed such tensions? It was, in fact, the seating arrangements in the parish church. To modern eyes this might appear somewhat innocuous, but the question of where people sat was actually highly significant. Those of higher status sat nearest the altar – literally nearest to God – while the lower orders formed ranks towards the back. This was a society where everyone was expected to know their place, but accepting or liking that place was a different matter. There was a constant jockeying for position as some felt aggrieved at the remoteness of their pew or, perhaps worse, were unseated by newcomers or social climbers.

In this case it was left to the churchwarden, a respected local yeoman farmer, to settle matters, which he did by setting out the new seating plan into his notebook. The churchwarden's name was John Gwin, part of a family who had come to the area in the 16th century. Remarkably, Gwin's book still survives, and its richness of detail allows a rare glimpse into the often hidden world of an 'ordinary' parish in 17th-century Wales – in many ways a more typical experience than that of the castle, the manor house or the large town.

COMMUNITY AND STATUS

In the 17th century, the parish of Llangwm consisted of two settlements, the larger Llangwm Uchaf (upper Llangwm) and Llangwm Isaf (lower Llangwm). Between them, they contained farmsteads, houses and the parish church. The population was small – probably less than 100 in the mid 17th century, but the lives of its inhabitants were closely intertwined. People lived cheek by jowl. They saw each other regularly, prayed together in church every Sunday and, despite the apparent cliché, probably did know much more about each other than we do of our neighbours today.

But even this tiny community reflected social patterns across the wider state, containing people of different levels of wealth and status. At the more prosperous end were men like John Gwin who were relatively well-off and, although they depended on employment for some of their income, also had some other private sources of money. Gwin was a member of what might be termed the 'middling sort'. He lived in a fairly substantial farmhouse of several rooms, with his wife, several children and servants. He was a man of modest wealth, able to afford the odd luxury like a silver tankard, for which he paid the princely sum of five pounds – more like five hundred in today's coin. According to an inventory of his 'ousel [household] stuff' Gwin's house – the 'Pwll' farm – contained several rooms, including a hall, loft and cellars and also a milk house and buttery. It was full of furniture, from functional items such as chairs and tables, to more decorative items such as a dresser. By the standards of the day, his was fairly sumptuous accommodation, as befitted his status as a respected local figure.

At the opposite end of the social spectrum, however, were the poorer sorts – servants, labourers and also those who eked out a meagre living as tenant farmers. Daily life and living conditions for people at either end of the social spectrum could be dramatically different. The houses of the poor in Wales were basic at best and little more than squalid at worst. Many Welsh cottages were small, smoky, sparsely furnished and might house animals living alongside their human inhabitants. There was no effective sanitation which, together with the presence of flies and vermin, made them the perfect breeding ground for disease. Whether Llangwm contained any of these poorest cottages is unclear, but they were certainly prevalent across rural Wales.

In close proximity were grander houses such as Allt-y-Bela – a magnificent towered house dating to the Renaissance and later improved by a wealthy and prominent Midlands wool merchant. It was a house that Gwin was very familiar with since it was owned by his friend, and there are many references to his visits there. The houses of the wealthy dotted the landscape, but few would have been as visible or imposing as Raglan Castle, seat of the Marquis of Worcester, a building that was to feature prominently in the lives of the inhabitants of Llangwm.

Despite the apparent gulf between wealthy and poor, though, it would be a mistake to suggest that the two groups did not interact. In fact, at all levels of society, networks of family, friends and acquaintances were enormously important. Gwin, for example, had a large network of acquaintances upon whose lands he indulged his hobby for grafting fruit trees. Then, as now, Monmouthshire was an ideal environment for apple and pear orchards, and cider-making was a common pursuit amongst those who could afford their own presses. Many pages of detailed notes attest to the diligence with which he set orchards and grafted trees on lands around Llangwm, and also to his obvious pride when the yields were good. Gwin, his sons and servants would also help out on the lands of his neighbours providing a source of labour at busy times – a favour doubtless reciprocated.

Equally important was the moral and religious obligation to support the poor and needy – a message thundered out from pulpits across the Principality. In times of hardship the Welsh community, as elsewhere in the country, provided

Raglan Castle, which featured prominently in the lives of the people of Llangwm

a sort of safety net. When sickness befell a member of a village, for example, evidence suggests that word could spread incredibly quickly, even within an hour or two. Family, friends and neighbours could all be relied upon to provide favoured remedies, advice or even physical care. Gwin's book makes note of many remedies, and also a suggestion that he passed them on to others, including servants and his 'landladies boy', suggesting that social status was no barrier to the sharing of valuable knowledge. In some cases, parish authorities might even pay a willing neighbour to move in with a sick person and look after them. Through collections under the Poor Law, organised through the parish church, the local community provided money to those experiencing financial hardships, as long as they were viewed as genuinely needy.

Nevertheless, as the seating dispute noted at the beginning amply demonstrates, the early modern village could also be a place of petty tensions, jealousies and quarrels. Evidence from other parishes in Wales at the time reveals the sorts of things that regularly aroused tempers and even led to prosecutions.

STICKS AND STONES...

Language, for example, was an extremely effective weapon, and a sharply-aimed insult could easily destroy a reputation. Consider the case of Gwenllian Williams of Glamorgan who, in 1702, publicly defamed Elizabeth David with the words 'thou art a common whore and doth keep a bawdy house". It was a similar suspicion of loose morals that perhaps provoked David Lewis of Llantrisant to publicly accuse his neighbour Walter Morgan of being 'a rogue and a shameless whoremaster'. Suspicions of crime could provoke equally hot words. Theft was clearly the impetus behind Rachel Reynolds broadside to Elizabeth Thomas, 'thou foul cheat, thou hast cheated me [out] of my pan'!

Even the very sense of social order which was supposed to encourage people to know their place could lead to discord. 1671, the same year as the dispute over church places, Gwin was forced to document the various responsibilities of the community for maintaining the church boundaries – a duty of all the people in the parish. By setting it down on paper, he clearly hoped to avoid potential squabbles, and give everyone a fair and equal responsibility.

FAITH AND THE WIDER WORLD

Until fairly recently it was still assumed that small towns and villages in the 17th century were relatively isolated places, with parish boundaries effectively forming the edge of the known world for inhabitants. But in reality, people were fairly mobile and in fact might travel fairly regularly outside the village to do business elsewhere, to visit, to find work or even, as Gwin did, to go shopping! From Llangwm, it was a relatively short ride on horseback to several notable market towns including Brecon, Abergavenny and Chepstow – a pattern mirrored across Wales where markets drew people from rural areas in to buy goods and services.

Importantly, it wasn't just within their own area, or even within Wales, that people travelled; the lure of bigger towns across the border often drew people outside. In North Wales, towns like Chester were a magnet for Welsh people. In mid Wales, Ludlow and Shropshire were large urban centres, and the sound of Welsh and English voices would have intermingled on market days. For Llangwm the comparatively huge town of Bristol was within reach. On the face of it this seems like a major undertaking. The village was located in a deeply rural area and, although it was close to some more substantial roads, could have taken up to several days' hard ride to reach on horseback. It was, however, also very close to the rivers Usk and Wye and, in fact, this was the main route by which Gwin regularly travelled to the city. Negotiating the sometimes treacherous waters first of the river and then of the Severn estuary in his family's boat, he made the journey to visit Bristol fair several times, purchasing everything from books to medicines. Sometimes he went alone, but sometimes took others. Whilst by no means everyone could travel, such examples remind us of the often surprising mobility of the early modern population.

The Severn estuary which John Gwin would have crossed by boat to go to Bristol fair

Neither were the people of Llangwm, in their deeply rural location, unaware of wider events in the world. Indeed, events often came uncomfortably close to them. In the 1640s, Monmouthshire was at the very centre of tensions between the crown and parliament. Gwin's father had worked as a steward for the estates of Henry Somerset, the first Marquis of Worcester, and he took over responsibility on his father's death. As the chief constable for Trelleck and

Raglan, he was peripherally involved in siege of Raglan castle (the family seat of the Worcesters) by Parliamentarian forces.

The Marquis was a prominent catholic and a staunch royalist. Gwin himself, however, had split loyalties. He was the churchwarden of the (by now Protestant) St Jerome's and the inclusion of passages from sermons by William Wroth – the founder of the earliest puritan church in Wales, at Llanvaches, tends to suggest that he had puritan tendencies. His wife's cousin was none other than Walter Craddock, the famous puritan 'divine', dispatched by Cromwell to educate the 'dark corners of the land', Wales included, in the true word of God. Craddock is actually buried in St Jerome's. But Gwin still owed his livelihood to the Catholic Worcesters. Also, his puritan beliefs did not prevent him from keeping notes of healing charms and prayers – including the 'adder stone' for sore eyes, or a cure for ague using imagery from the Lord's Prayer. Clearly, religion was a matter of tension, even in the smallest villages in Wales.

Raglan castle

This single example actually illustrates well the complex religious situation in Wales at this time, and the ways in which individuals had to reconcile the need to conform to the law of the land, with their own private beliefs. Traditionally, Wales has been viewed as a country which accepted Protestantism after the Reformation, but still retained many elements of pre-Reformation beliefs and practices, such as saint's days, holy wells and healing charms. Every Sunday, the congregation at St Jerome's attended Anglican services but did so in a church still retaining a spectacularly intricate carved roodscreen dating from medieval times – when the church had been Catholic. This was significant at a time when most churches in Protestant England and Wales had been stripped of what was regarded as Catholic superstitious idolatry and imagery.

LLANGWM – A TYPICAL WELSH VILLAGE?

Located almost on the very border with England, how 'Welsh' was it? On this matter there is little doubt; Llangwm was very firmly Welsh. Its inhabitants, in common with the vast majority of the population in Wales, and even in South Wales at the time, would have spoken Welsh as their first language. They were perhaps more likely to be bilingual, with some fluency in English, although even this cannot be assumed. Gwin himself clearly spoke Welsh (although, as was common, he wrote in English) and sometimes noted the Welsh terms for things he mentioned in his book. When recording his mother-in-law's last words, ('O Duw Kymmer Vi' – 'Oh God, come for me') he used the vernacular Welsh rather than translating it.

In many other ways, Llangwm reflected patterns familiar across Wales. Its inhabitants were subject to the same social and economic stresses and strains as those faced by their compatriots in Pembrokeshire or Caernarfonshire. In religious terms they faced the same questions of belief and spirituality as did the population of Britain in the turbulent years of the mid 17th century. Despite its isolated, rural location, Llangwm was part of a much bigger picture, a network of small hamlets, villages, parishes and towns which formed the geographical worldview of people at the time, and around which goods, people and information all moved with surprising fluidity.

If Llangwm was typical, then, it was certainly not dull. It presents us with Wales in miniature, a small glimpse into the ways that our ancestors lived, worshipped, experienced and interacted with each other. As such, it merits a place as a landmark, even an icon, in Welsh history.

And what of John Gwin himself? Can we consider him typical? In many ways no. Gwin was unusual in that he was relatively wealthy, well-connected, and had positions of prominence both in the community and the county. He was also literate, something which marked him out. But it is this very literacy that has allowed us to see his world through his own eyes. Typical he may not have been. But in every sense of the word he was exceptional.

Further Reading:
Geraint H. Jenkins, *The Foundations of Modern Wales, 1642–1780* (2002)

9

THE CONVENIENT VILLAINS – LLANTRITHYD PLACE

Lloyd Bowen

You have probably never heard of Llantrithyd Place. Today it lies derelict and ruined in fields a few miles south of the A48 between Cardiff and Cowbridge. Not a very promising candidate for an important building and place in Welsh history. In its very obscurity, however, lies the story of what was once Wales's most powerful ruling class: the gentry.

Glimpses of its former glories can be seen in the extensive ivy-clad ruins, but enter the small church only yards away from the broken walls and you are confronted with striking evidence for the faded significance of Llantrithyd Place and its residents. Here is a massive 16th-century family altar tomb dominating the tiny interior. It retains its colourful paint and gilded detailing and shows a man in armour lying next to his wife, both with their hands together in prayer. Above them are two more figures kneeling in prayer. Around the base are images of children. The monument is capped by a magnificent family coat of arms. This is bling on a serious scale, a display of wealth, ancestry and magnificence which suggests how these figures who once occupied Llantrithyd Place dominated the area in the 16th and 17th centuries.

The figures on the tomb are John ap Thomas Bassett and Anthony Mansel and their wives and children. The men were members of the gentry order, a class of super-rich landowners which held the levers of power in Wales between the end of the middle ages and the beginnings of industrial Wales. They were the country's movers and shakers for three centuries, and their towering significance invests buildings like Llantrithyd Place with a lasting importance. Yet we have largely forgotten them and their houses. Why?

FORGETTING LLANTRITHYD PLACE AND THE POLITICS OF THE PAST

Here we encounter aspects of the politics of our past. The Welsh like to think of themselves in terms of the 'common man'. The *real* Welshman is working class, radical, liberal, even socialist, nonconformist and Welsh-speaking or bilingual. The Welsh gentry were none of these things, hence they are often seen as not being really Welsh. They are the convenient villains of Welsh history – English-speaking and distant from the ordinary folk (*y werin*) whose labour they exploited, whose lands they stole and whose culture they betrayed. We want to forget about the gentry, to treat them as alien to our national story. That is one reason why you have never heard of Llantrithyd Place.

And yet if we forget the Welsh gentry we do a disservice to the remarkable social, cultural and political impact of figures such as those who built and lived in Llantrithyd Place. Few would argue that they were charitable philanthropists with the best interests of their community always in mind. However, they are a key part of our history and are responsible for some of our greatest buildings and cultural landmarks. They were also formative influences in shaping Wales's political and religious past. The ruins of Llantrithyd Place offer a vivid and illuminating insight into the Welsh gentry and their world, and thus into a key, but often neglected, part of our history.

Llantrithyd church

Llantrithyd church interior

ORIGINS: JOHN AP THOMAS BASSETT AND THE REFORMATION

Llantrithyd Place is associated with three gentry families: the Bassetts, the Mansels and the Aubreys. Tradition has it that the house was built in 1546 by John ap Thomas Bassett, probably on the site of an older building. He was a member of the family who owned the nearby castle of Beaupre. As their name suggests, the Bassetts were of English origin, but the family had been resident in Glamorgan since the 13th century and had become thoroughly Welsh. The house he built consisted of a double-pile main block with adjoining wings, forming three sides of a courtyard which was open to the west.

Bassett was an upwardly mobile man who trained as a lawyer and used his wealth to buy land. He purchased extensive estates near Llantrithyd including Peterson-super-Ely, Bonvilston and Talyfan, close to Cowbridge. These purchases gave him considerable power and prestige in the locality, and laid the foundations of the future influence of Llantrithyd Place in South Wales. Bassett entered the service of Queen Catherine Parr and was involved in the distribution of land and riches from the monasteries dissolved by Henry VIII. The profound upheavals of the Reformation and the high politics of the English Court are mixed into the mortar of Llantrithyd Place. Bassett sat in parliament on three occasions, and died while representing Glamorgan during Queen Mary's reign in 1551, leaving money in his will for the 'reparation of my house of Llantrithed'.

THE COMING OF THE AUBREY FAMILY

He gave Llantrithyd to his daughter, Elizabeth, who married Anthony Mansel, a member of another prominent gentry family in Glamorgan. It was she who built part of the magnificent monument in Llantrithyd church commemorating her parents. Five of Anthony and Elizabeth's children died young, including, crucially at this time, all three potential male heirs. However, the couple did have two surviving daughters, Mary and 'Cissill'. They were very tempting marriage prospects as co-heiresses of the huge Llantrithyd estates. Mary caught the eye of another successful lawyer, Dr William Aubrey of Breconshire, who concluded a match between her and his second son, Thomas, in 1586. Henceforth Llantrithyd Place would be associated with the name Aubrey. They are the reason the nearby hamlet is 'Tre-Aubrey', and why the pub on the A48 to the north is 'The Aubrey Arms'.

Thomas Aubrey moved into the house where life with the mother-in-law was not always easy or harmonious, particularly after Anthony Mansel died in 1604. In 1605 a lawsuit was brought by a household servant, Matthew Rosser, which accused Aubrey of assaulting him. Rosser was employed principally by Elizabeth Mansel, and she was less than pleased with her son-in-law's conduct, observing, 'Son, you never learned this of your father-in-law'. She was a strong woman of independent means, and concord does not seem to have come to the house until she died in 1607 and Thomas Aubrey had unhindered authority in Llantrithyd.

A UNIQUE RECORD: THE HOUSEHOLD ACCOUNTS OF LLANTRITHYD PLACE

We know more about Sir Thomas Aubrey (as he became) and his house than almost any of his peers among the Welsh gentry because he left behind some unique documents. These are now housed among some miscellaneous materials (including an unidentified but centuries-old box of hair) at the National Archives in Kew. These constitute a set of paper household accounts kept by Sir Thomas during the 1620s and 1630s. They record expenditure on a wide variety of goods and services, and give us an unrivalled picture of the household dynamics at Llantrithyd in this period.

These documents tell us that the house and its gardens were a major (and expensive) priority for Aubrey. This was not simply a home for Sir Thomas and his family. It also functioned as a symbol of his wealth and pre-eminence in the local community. The house and its environs were the setting in which he could demonstrate the qualities of a gentleman as husband, father, employer (doubtless Rosser would disagree!), landlord and local magnate.

Aubrey's accounts show frequent payments to joiners, glaziers, tilers, masons, plasterers, carpenters, thatchers and workmen. There was remodelling and new building going on throughout the period of the accounts, including the building of a 'ladies chamber' which was varnished with 4 lbs of broken amber. Keeping up with the Joneses (literally in his case as there was a gentry family of that name not too far away) was not the invention of the consumer age.

Although there was no photographer from *OK! Magazine* on the horizon, it was necessary that Aubrey was seen adopting the latest interior fashions and living like a cultured gentleman. In May 1623, for example, he paid a Mr Heath of Gloucester for a variety of cushions to adorn the chambers at Llantrithyd, and also had the beds recovered with silk and calico.

Aubrey created a 'grand gallery' at Llantrithyd measuring 68 feet by 24 feet to impress his visitors. In this space he built a magnificent new fireplace in 1627, bringing wood from Bristol and importing alabaster at nearby Aberthaw.

Here the accounts allow us to catch a glimpse of a workman who can stand for the many nameless and faceless labourers that maintained Llantrithyd in a state of splendour over the centuries. Aubrey details weekly payments of 10 shillings (a not inconsiderable sum) to a man only known as 'Christopher' for constructing the fireplace. This was not a simple affair. The fireplace possessed two figures of Justice and Mercy in veined marble and was surmounted by a large heraldic shield displaying Aubrey's arms along with those of the Mansels and Bassetts.

The Bassett-Mansel Tomb

Llantrithyd Place is located in a fertile and picturesque part of the Vale of Glamorgan, and its parks and gardens were also important for displaying the cultured qualities of its owner. It did not disappoint. Llantrithyd Place was described in 1591 as a 'fair domain, with parks, warrens and orchards and groves of goodly trees in abundance'. It possessed walled gardens and terracing descending to rectangular fishponds, a rarity at this time, and which were linked by a canalized stream. Sir Thomas cultivated an orchard of nectarine and cherry trees, even importing some from London. His impressive deer park remains a feature of the area with the commercial production of venison continuing in this ancient setting.

A CENTRE OF CULTURE AND ENTERTAINMENT

Aubrey's accounts also provide some fascinating detail on the kinds of cultural and social activities which occurred at and around Llantrithyd. Visitors called constantly and had to be fed and entertained. One notable visitor was the Lord Deputy of Ireland, Oliver, 4th Baron St John, who called at Llantrithyd when returning from Ireland in May 1622. The sumptuous entertainment he received included a hogshead of expensive claret wine from Bristol, a sturgeon, £10 of imported sweetmeats and other delicacies, and £20-worth of other luxury items. The average annual wage for the servants at Llantrithyd Place was between £1 and £2.

Music was important at Llantrithyd, and Sir Thomas retained his own harpist, 'George', who was particularly busy during times of celebration such as Christmas and New Year. Itinerant musicians were also entertained here including a 'blind harper' at Christmas 1632 and a Scottish 'taborer'. The gentlemen of the surrounding area also sent their musicians to entertain at Llantrithyd, who included harpists, trumpeters and fiddlers.

Sir Thomas was raised in a thoroughly hybrid Anglo-Welsh culture. He had Welsh verse composed for him as a youth in 1600, and he himself patronised Welsh itinerant poets who performed at Llantrithyd. It is perhaps telling, however, that in 1633 he recorded the five shillings he paid 'unto the Welsh poet' – the use of the adjective 'Welsh' suggesting that such entertainment was unusual or different from the usual fare. Indeed, alongside more traditional Welsh cultural pursuits we also find newer entertainments recorded among his papers. The accounts tell us for the first time that Shakespeare's old company of players, The King's Men, visited Wales in 1621, with Aubrey paying them 20 shillings after a performance just down the road at St Nicholas.

ROYALIST REFUGE: LLANTRITHYD PLACE AND THE CIVIL WARS

The vivid picture of gentry life at Llantrithyd Place begins to fade as the dark clouds of civil war gather on the horizon. Sir Thomas's last recorded accounts are dated in 1637 and he died in November 1641. His son, John, was a passionate supporter of Charles I and a beacon of royalism in South Wales. Llantrithyd Place became a haven for royalist refugees during the civil wars, with the future Archbishop of Canterbury Gilbert Sheldon, the Irish Archbishop James Ussher, and the principal of Jesus College, Oxford, Francis Mansell, sheltering there from the parliamentarians. One London royalist who took refuge at Llantrithyd Place in 1652 clearly saw it as a haven from the political and social turmoil elsewhere, describing it as a 'Welsh paradise for building, situation, pleasure and plenty'.

John Aubrey suffered for his allegiance to the king, but was rewarded for his loyalty at the Restoration with a baronetcy. The family's star was rising again.

His son, another John (the second baronet), was a cultured man with an interest in the new learning emerging from groups such as the Royal Society. He corresponded with the polymath Welshman Edward Lhuyd and sponsored the publication of academic texts.

ABANDONING LLANTRITHYD: THE ABSENTEE GENTRY

This John Aubrey's principal significance, however, lies in the fact that in the 1690s he acquired through marriage the Buckinghamshire estate of Boarstall. The lure of what was seen as a more refined English estate closer to the social hub of London was considerable. As early as 1693 he had resolved to 'live one halfe yeare in Wales, and the other at Boarstall'. As time went on the family's residence at Llantrithyd became increasingly brief and intermittent. During the course of the 18th century they developed into wholly English gentlemen and were notorious absentees from their Welsh lands, which were administered on their behalf by stewards. Llantrithyd was abandoned in the early 19th century.

The Aubreys faded from the collective memory and history of Wales as their ancestral home crumbled into ruinous neglect. They had fulfilled their role as one of the villains of Welsh history.

Few of the inhabitants of Llantrithyd Place come across as particularly commendable or attractive individuals. Sir Thomas was described colourfully by one adversary as 'a man of a very high and haughty disposition given much to contention and of an unsociable carriage of himself towards such as he doth converse withal… A great oppressor of his poor neighbours and of sundry others'.

Clearly he was an ambitious and ruthless individual as were many of his gentry counterparts. But this is not the whole picture. Aubrey was also a dispenser of charity, a patron of the arts, a supporter of Welsh culture, a powerful and respected local justice and a man of culture, education and refinement. Like all of us he was a complex figure, not simply the caricature villain portrayed by his adversaries and later generations. We should not judge such men by the standards of our age, for then we do violence to the real shape and meaning of our past. We may not like it, but Llantrithyd Place is as integral to, and as emblematic of, our history as the more familiar industrial heritage of our towns and cities. The tumbling bones of the mansion at Llantrithyd, just like the petrified winding towers of our collieries, are part of the raw material of our collective past.

Further Reading:
Lloyd Bowen, *Family and Society in Early Stuart Glamorgan: The Household Accounts of Sir Thomas Aubrey of Llantrithyd, c.1565–1641* (2006)

The ruins of Llantrithyd Place

10

MIGHT AND SPITE –
THE FORMER MIDDLETON HALL
ESTATE

Lowri Ann Rees

In May 2000 the National Botanic Garden of Wales opened to the public. Since then, the place has seen its ups and downs, with fluctuating visitor numbers and even the threat of closure in 2004. Nonetheless, in 2006 *Western Mail* readers voted the Great Glasshouse as their number one Wonder of Wales, a sure sign of the structure's iconic status. It is the largest single spanned glasshouse in the world, showcasing a dazzling display of Mediterranean climate plants. The site as a whole spreads across 560 acres of beautiful countryside, on which grow more than 8,000 varieties of plants.

The garden's mission is to foster research and lifelong learning, conserve biodiversity, promote sustainability and cater for the needs of visitors. Being the most visited garden in Wales makes it an important place. However, the garden's popularity also draws attention to the fact that Wales has a rich garden heritage, with an array of parklands and woodlands open to visitors. Many of these sites have long histories, and the NBGW is no exception. Indeed, it is very fitting that the site between the villages of Porthyrhyd and Llanarthne, on the cusp of the Tywi Valley, was chosen as the home of the NBGW, as more than 200 years ago, another enchanting garden had just been established there.

THE MIDDLETON HALL ESTATE

The history of the Middleton Hall estate stretches back to the early 17th century. During this time, the landlord, Henry Middleton, built a substantial house on the estate. This building must have been of considerable size, as

Middleton Hall, before the National Botanic Gardens was even a dream
(Crown copyright: Royal Commission on Ancient and Historical Monuments, Wales)

according to the Hearth Tax records of 1670, it contained a total of 17 hearths. The Middleton family continued to reside on the estate until financial difficulties forced them to sell in order to settle debts. Towards the end of the 18th century the estate was purchased by a newly wealthy banker and merchant, who was to make the most visible mark on Middleton Hall.

William Paxton (c.1744–1824) was born in Edinburgh. His father was chief clerk to the wine-merchant and Lord Provost of Edinburgh, Archibald Stewart. Although a Scotsman, Paxton spent much of his childhood in London, following the family's relocation due to his father's work commitments. At the age of twelve, Paxton joined the Royal Navy as a Captain's servant. He soon rose through the ranks to become midshipman, but his career path diverted when he became an officer on a private British merchant ship bound for India. It was there that he made his fortune. Having trained to become an assayer, analysing minerals and ores to determine their worth, Paxton became assay master at Fort William in Bengal. He later set up his own agency house, called Paxton, Cockerell and Trail, which became most successful, with a branch set up in London. Due to British expansion in South Asia, predominantly through the activities of the East India Company, there were opportunities to amass considerable fortunes. Paxton was not alone, and even some Welshmen succeeded in profiteering from the colonial rule of India.

Having secured his fortune, Paxton returned to Britain during the 1780s. With a new wife and growing family to provide for, Paxton was keen to purchase a landed estate. Buying a landed estate was also a way Paxton could try to climb up the social ladder and integrate into the ranks of the landed elite. It appears that his sights were set on Carmarthenshire. In 1785 he had expressed an interest in the 3,048-acre Taliaris estate near Llandeilo, but on the day of the sale was outbid by Lord Robert Seymour. However, another estate was up for sale in the county, and in 1789 Paxton purchased Middleton Hall. Between 1793–95 a grand new mansion was built, described as 'one of the best built, and most magnificent houses in Wales' and 'a truly magnificent mansion… seated on a prominent elevated spot, in the midst of a beautiful valley, branching off to the eastward of the river Towey, between a chain of hills to Llandilo and the sea, forming a grand and highly picturesque scenery'. The new Middleton Hall had been designed by the architect Samuel Pepys Cockerell in the neo-classical style, complete with a grand and imposing portico. The interior of the mansion was equally as elaborate, and decorated in the latest fashions. The new mansion also had water closets, with water supplied from a roof top cistern, which was fed by a reservoir built on the side of a nearby hill. This was an innovative feature at the time, and few country houses in Wales could boast such technology.

The modernization did not stop with the mansion, as located on the estate was an ice house. This was a building designed to store ice and preserve food in the days before refrigerators. Although this was a feature of many large country estates at the time, with another local example to be found at Dinefwr near Llandeilo, the Middleton Hall ice house is classed as one of the best examples of its kind in Wales, and can still be seen to this day.

GARDEN INNOVATIONS AT MIDDLETON HALL

During his 35 years as landlord of Middleton Hall, Paxton oversaw the transformation of the parkland surrounding his new mansion. In addition to building a series of service buildings and a stable block, a double walled garden encompassing more than three acres of land was constructed. The double walled garden was not a common feature found in Welsh gardens. An outer wall constructed of stone, and an inner wall constructed of brick helped create a milder micro-climate within the garden. This extended the growing season of a variety of fruits and vegetables. A glasshouse was built within the double walled garden, and via a sophisticated system of under floor heating, peaches, along with a range of other fruits, were grown.

Paxton also developed ornamental parklands and woodlands, a necklace of lakes, damns, sluices and a stunning waterfall at the site of present day Pont Felin

National Botanic Garden of Wales

Gât. The artist Thomas Horner was commissioned to capture these features in a series of watercolour paintings dated 1815. On discovering that water with a high mineral content was found on his estate, Paxton built a bath house for the exclusive use of the family. However, Paxton ensured that this water was to be piped to the outskirts of the parkland wall so that visitors could also take to the waters. Visitors travelled from far and wide to sample the Middleton Hall waters, many finding accommodation at nearby Llanarthne. Such innovations in garden technology and landscaping set a precedent for years to come, and provided inspiration for the establishment of the NBGW 200 years later.

PAXTON'S TOWER

Another building on the Middleton Hall estate of great symbolism is Paxton's Tower. The thirty-six foot high, gothic three-sided tower was built during the first decade of the 19th century. Having already requested the architect Samuel Pepys Cockerell design his new home, Paxton turned to him again to draw up plans for the tower. Paxton's motives for erecting such a building continue to be debated to this day. As the tower was built not long after Paxton's spectacular defeat in the infamous 1802 Carmarthenshire county election, one theory suggests he wanted to emphasise that the contest had not ruined him financially.

BOOZE FOR VOTES

Paxton was billed for more than £15,000 following his treating of voters in an attempt to secure their electoral support. A total of 11,070 breakfasts, 36,901 dinners, 6,842 suppers, 25,275 gallons of ale and porter, 11,074 bottles of spirits, 8,879 bottles of porter, 4,060 bottles of sherry, 509 bottles of cider, £18 18 shillings worth of milk punch, £54 worth of mulled wine and 4,521 horse hire items were charged.

Another theory suggests that Paxton funded the construction of the tower with money promised for the building of a much needed bridge across the river Tywi. Therefore the tower was meant to serve as a visible reminder to the people of Carmarthen who failed to support Paxton during his ill-fated foray into Carmarthenshire politics. This is why the tower is sometimes called 'Tŵr Sbeit' (the tower of spite).

However, the most likely explanation is that Paxton had the tower built in order to conform to the landscaping trends of the day. It was fashionable to build follies on estates, utilising architectural feature in order to enhance the landscape. Paxton dedicated the tower to the memory of Horatio Nelson, killed during the Battle of Trafalgar in 1805. Originally called 'Nelson's Tower', engraved tablets commemorating Nelson in Welsh, Latin and English were placed on each of the three sides of the tower.

The largest single spanned glasshouse in the world

PAXTON'S CONTRIBUTION TO THE LOCAL AREA

The Middleton Hall estate was transformed by Paxton, however, he also had a wider impact in the community. To name a few examples, Paxton established a charity school at Llanarthne, donated land on a lease for the building of Bethlehem Baptist Chapel in Porthyrhyd, and subscribed a substantial £1,000 towards the building of a canal along the Gwendraeth valley and improvements to Kidwelly harbour. Perhaps the most visible mark made on the Welsh landscape was the regeneration of the seaside town of Tenby. From the mid-18th century, seaside resorts became increasingly fashionable, especially with the curative properties of sea bathing being promoted. Towards the end of the century, restrictions on travel to the Continent were imposed by the French Revolutionary Wars, therefore a greater number of the elite opted to holiday at home, which contributed to the rise of the coastal resorts. Landed families flocked to Wales to enjoy the benefits of sea bathing, but also the accompanying social rounds of balls, parties and assemblies. Travel writers published descriptive accounts of tours across Wales, portraying a romanticised image of the country to entice visitors. In this climate, other seaside resorts developed – Aberystwyth was known as 'the Brighton of Wales', and Swansea was also transformed into a fashionable bathing place.

Landowners played an important role in the development of seaside resorts. In addition to Tenby, another Welsh example is the transformation of Llandudno through the help of the Mostyn family during the mid-19th century. Tenby was a town that had fallen into decline, but with Paxton's financial support and initiative, it became a vibrant and fashionable resort. Crowds of visitors were drawn to the town, boosting the local economy.

Following a visit to Tenby in 1805, Paxton again commissioned the architect Samuel Pepys Cockerell, requesting the designing of a bathhouse in Tenby. By 1810, the *Carmarthen Journal* proudly declared that the Tenby baths were open 'for the conveniency of the Gentry, and others who visit this charming Bathing Place'. Visitors could bathe in one of the two swimming baths or submerge themselves in either the cold, warm or vapour baths. However,

WIDENING STREETS AND BROADENING MINDS

Paxton built several lodging houses to cater for the steady influx of visitors. He also funded projects to widen streets within the town and build new roads to allow for easier access. He was even a key subscriber of a new theatre in Frog Street in 1810. The theatre proved a success during the early decades of the 19th century, and attracted professional companies. There was room for 80 spectators in the pit, 120 in the boxes and 160 in the gallery.

the social aspect of the seaside resort was also important, therefore within the bathhouse was a grand billiard room and drawing room with spectacular views across the bay and out to sea.

However, Paxton's projects were not of exclusive benefit to elite visitors to Tenby. A major contribution was bringing a supply of fresh water to the town, thereby improving the quality of life and general health of the urban populace. The travel writer Richard Fenton praised Paxton 'the worthy knight' (for he had been honoured by the King in 1803), exclaiming 'the town is indebted to the spirit and liberality of Sir William Paxton for having effectually remedied the most essential of its defects, the want of water'. This was not the first project of its kind that Paxton had undertaken. During his time as Mayor of Carmarthen in 1803 he was instrumental in plans to improve the water supply to the town. The plans involved the installation of iron pipes to replace the previously used wooden ones, which unsurprisingly leaked.

IMPERIAL WEALTH

As highlighted by Professor Huw Bowen in *A New History of Wales*, the first book in this series, Wales does not feature very prominently in histories of the British Empire. However, that is not to say that Wales did not see the influx of wealth into the Welsh economy through imperial exploitation. The development of Middleton Hall and the far-reaching effects of Paxton's projects highlight this. Money generated in India paid for the Middleton Hall estate and the building of Paxton's new home. That same fortune was pumped into the Welsh economy, be it through the funding of urban regeneration in Carmarthen and Tenby, subscriptions to canal building and improvements schemes, through charitable donations or during election campaigns, especially the notoriously expensive 1802 Carmarthenshire county election. This influx of wealth left its mark on the local area, and should not be forgotten, especially as the source of wealth came from British colonial expansion overseas at a considerable cost to human life.

CONCLUSION

By acknowledging the importance of the site of Paxton's former estate, we highlight the important garden heritage that Wales possesses. William Paxton's role was also significant. During his time at Middleton Hall, he enacted several improvements. Some were purely cosmetic, whilst others improved the quality of the land. Acknowledging the importance of Middleton Hall also acknowledges the impact Paxton had on south-west Wales. This impact can be seen even to this day. Paxton's Tower still stands and is a striking feature in the landscape, which can be seen for miles. Tenby remains a bustling seaside resort which relies on the crowds of tourists it attracts year on year. The blue plaques scattered around the town to commemorate Paxton's projects are a nod to his urban regeneration efforts. The ruins and remains of the once spectacular Middleton Hall estate provided the foundations for the establishment of a national botanic garden in Wales in the new Millennium. Therefore, considering these wide ranging factors, the former Middleton Hall estate site is arguably an important place in Wales – a site that has evolved over the last 200 years, but a site that continues to display the same ethos of innovation and improvement.

Further reading:
Andrew Sclater (ed.), *The National Botanic Garden of Wales* (2000)

Middleton Hall today

11

POETIC BATTLEGROUND – PUMLUMON AND THE ELENYDD

Martin Wright

> That all the Cambrian hills, which high'st their heads doe beare
> With most obsequious showes of low subjected feare,
> Should to thy greatness stoupe...

... is how Michael Drayton addressed Pumlumon in his great topographical work of 1622, the *Poly-Olbion*. His assertion that 'all the neighbouring hills Plynillimon obey' might, however, be considered unduly modest. The mountain's great ridge commands not just the surrounding topography; rather, it has dictated the course of Welsh history. O.M. Edwards asserted over a hundred years ago that Wales was a 'land of mountains' that have 'determined throughout its history what the direction and method of its progress were to be'. Pumlumon may not be the highest, or the most dramatic of them. It is, though, without doubt the most important.

Pen Pumlumon Fawr, the highest of Pumlumon's five peaks, is located roughly halfway between Aberystwyth and Llanidloes. At 2,467 feet, it is the highest point between Snowdonia and the Brecon Beacons. On a clear day, from the Bronze Age cairn on its summit, the mountain's primacy quickly becomes apparent. All of Wales unfolds to the gaze. To the west, Snowdonia is linked to the Preseli by the great arc of Cardigan Bay. To the east, the Berwyn and Aran ranges draw the eye round to the English border, along which the Long Mynd, the Breidden and the Radnor Forest connect the view to the Black Mountains, which in turn merge into the great South Wales escarpment. No one who has stood upon the summit of Pumlumon and studied this view would deny that, regardless of its measured height, the mountain is the true apex of Wales.

MABINOGILAND

It was from Pumlumon, in the story of Culhwch and Olwen, that Cai and Bedwyr sat (to use the English of Charlotte Guest) 'in the highest wind that ever was in the world', and saw the smoke rising from the fire of Dillus Farfawc. They then fell upon him in his sleep, threw him into a pit, plucked out his beard with a pair of wooden tweezers and killed him. Pumlumon is no ordinary place.

BORDERLAND

More prosaically, the guide who took George Borrow, author of *Wild Wales*, to Pumlumon's summit in 1854 questioned 'whether there is a higher hill in the world'. It may have been the highest hill in his world. Borrow, though, with his customary air of superiority, commented that it did not appear particularly grand from its immediate southern slopes. This may be true, but as Borrow's guide explained, this is because the mountain rises in the south from an already considerable elevation. Indeed, Pumlumon's pre-eminent position in Welsh topography cannot be understood without remembering that it is but the culmination of a much greater tract of upland that stretches from the Tywi and Llandovery in the south to the Dyfi and Machynlleth in the north. The west of this region is bounded by the River Teifi and the settlements of Lampeter, Tregaron and Pontrhydfendigaid, and its eastern boundaries are set by the Wye and Irfon valleys, and the settlements of Rhayader and Llanwrtyd.

Within this quadrangle lies roughly 800 square miles of what some have called the 'Green Desert of Wales'. The features of this great wilderness include the most remote of all Welsh hills, Drygarn Fawr, the presence of which has been accentuated since the Bronze Age by the huge beehive cairns on its summit. The land is not exceptionally high. Only in a few places do the contours break 2,000 feet. It is, however, unremittingly desolate. Except where the plateau is unexpectedly broken by wild valleys such as the Pysgotwr or the Doethie, or covered by modern conifer plantations, it is uniformly open and windswept. From its fastness flow some of the great rivers of Wales and Britain: the Wye, the Severn, the Rheidol, the Teifi, the Tywi, the Cothi, the Elan and the Irfon. This stretch of land is most often referred to as the 'Cambrian Mountains'. The real name for the greater part of it, though, is the Elenydd.

The name is ancient. In another of the Mabinogi, the story of Math, the magician Gwydion drives a herd of swine he has stolen from Pryderi, king of Dyfed, back to Math, king of Gwynedd, across the Elenydd – the land that effectively separates the two kingdoms. This would suggest that the name was used by the very earliest of Welsh people. Gerald of Wales also uses the term

Pumlumon from the south
(Martin Wright)

in his topographical works, the *Journey Through Wales* and the *Description of Wales*, written around the end of the 12th century. Significantly, both the *Mabinogi* and Gerald refer to Elenydd as a borderland, and it is in this respect that its primary influence upon Welsh history has been felt.

The Elenydd is the great watershed of Wales. It divides east from west and north from south. Its own core defines the furthermost reaches of the economic and administrative influence that has historically emanated from the population centres on its margins. Five of the historic counties of Wales – Cardiganshire, Carmarthenshire, Brecknockshire, Radnorshire and Montgomeryshire – are separated by it; their borders dictated by the most remote geographical features in Wales. Its dividing influence, however, runs much deeper than mere politics or administration. It is also cultural and linguistic. Its presence has been a major factor in the separate evolution of the different cultures that characterise North and South Wales, and helps to explain the difficulties that have so often beset attempts to create national unity in Welsh history.

There is, however, another dimension to the influence of the Elenydd upon Wales. If its presence has divided the nation, it has also worked to preserve native Welsh culture from the anglicising influences that have emanated from the east. Its mountainous geography so effectively slowed the march of the English language that by 1801, when almost nine out of ten of the inhabitants of Radnorshire were English speakers, Cardiganshire, across the hills, remained a bastion of the Welsh language. In the same year less than one in ten of that county's population had learnt English, and despite the spread of bilingualism during the 19th century, the counties west of the Elenydd remained a heartland of the Welsh language. It might thus be argued that one of the primary factors in the survival of the Welsh language has been the Elenydd.

HEARTLAND

It is perhaps puzzling that a region of such historical importance has not occupied a more central position in Welsh national consciousness. Even its name seems to have lapsed into disuse after the medieval period. In 1903 the travel writer A.G. Bradley remarked upon the inexplicability of such a compact, distinct and historically influential mountain range apparently having no commonly recognised name, and he advocated the revival of what he anglicised as 'Ellineth'. It took the best part of a century for the idea to catch on, but during recent decades 'Elenydd' has gradually been restored to the topographical lexicon of Wales. Even officialdom has now adopted it, in the form of an 'Elenydd Designated Special Area of Conservation'.

This resurrection is worthy of celebration, for it is not only as a borderland that this region has influenced Welsh history. Paradoxically, the Elenydd and Pumlumon comprise the true heartland of Wales. It is significant that Cistercian monks chose the haven of the Elenydd for the site of one of their most important Abbeys: that founded under the patronage of Rhys ap Gruffudd, prince of Deheubarth, at Strata Florida in 1164. As another article in this book has shown, the sanctuary provided by the surrounding mountains created the conditions for a remarkable flowering of Welsh culture in the medieval period. It was here that *Brut y Tywysogion* – the most important of all sources for early Welsh history – was compiled. The wealth that enabled such cultural achievements was directly derived from the sheepwalks of the great Elenydd upland. In other words, without the influence of the Elenydd our knowledge of the early history of Wales would be greatly diminished.

It was not just the monks of Strata Florida whose culture flourished in the haven of the region's hills. The poet Dafydd ap Gwilym was certainly no cenobite. He was born around 1320 at Brogynin, a *plas* situated among the western foothills of Pumlumon, and his exquisite *cywyddau*, with their intertwining themes of love and nature, were a direct product of the mountain environment that was his *bro*. Although he travelled widely throughout Wales during his (to judge by his work) amorous and colourful life, he was (according to tradition at least) ultimately buried at Strata Florida. Arguably the greatest of Welsh poets, then, was a son of Pumlumon.

OUTLAWS AND APOSTLES

Dafydd ap Gwilym provides just one example of the culture that has flourished across the centuries in this great heartland. The region and its bordering communities have produced such diverse and influential figures as the outlaw Thomas Jones (Twm Sion Catti, c. 1530–1609), the educationalist Kilsby Jones (1813–1889) and the politician Henry Richard (the 'Apostle of Peace', 1812–1888). It rivals any other part of Wales in the creation of the culture of the werin, and, although the last century has been increasingly hostile to the cultural life of the uplands, the communities around Pumlumon and the Elenydd remain among the most significant cradles of rural Welsh culture.

INSPIRATION

In addition to nourishing and sustaining a rich native culture, the Elenydd has also inspired those who have come from afar. In 1811 Percy Bysshe Shelley walked from England to its heart at Cwm Elan, where he stayed at a mansion owned by his uncle. 'Astonished by the grandeur of the scenery', as he put it, he subsequently attempted to buy the nearby house of Nantgwyllt and settle

King of the Mountains – Elvis lives on the A44 on Pumlumon

there. Shelley was, in his own words, 'not wholly uninfluenced' by the magic of the place. There is an element, therefore, of sublime Welsh upland beauty in what would generally be considered to be the quintessentially English work of one of Britain's greatest romantic poets.

Over a century later, a visionary of a wholly different type was inspired by the uplands of Pumlumon. Reginald George Stapledon was a Cambridge-educated botanist who, in 1919, was appointed first Director of the Welsh Plant Breeding Station at Aberystwyth. Drawing upon the uplands of Pumlumon and the Elenydd as inspiration and scientific resource in equal measure, he developed new methods of grassland management that have subsequently influenced agricultural methods worldwide. He also developed ideas about land use that have played a significant role in shaping the way that we relate to this most basic of resources.

In *The Land Now and Tomorrow* (1935) Stapledon was among the first in Britain to advocate the extensive use of land for social amenity. His vision for Britain's first National Park was directly inspired by Pumlumon, and the book contains detailed proposals for such a park to be established on the mountain. His plans included driving a tarmac road through the wild valley of Hengwm, along which he envisaged the building of tennis courts and other sporting amenities. Modern wilderness advocates may well consider them alarming. His vision nevertheless contributed to the establishment of national parks in Britain – a process that opened much of the nation's countryside to its people for the first time in recent history. It is ironic, though, that Stapledon's own ideal national park on the slopes of Pumlumon was never created.

RESOURCE

There is a great tension between Stapledon's vision of the land as an amenity for all and the attitude of those who see it as something to exploit, and its outcomes may be clearly observed in the landscape of Pumlumon and the Elenydd. Exploitation of this heartland has been a central feature of Welsh history, alongside which the 19th-century South Wales coal boom appears no more than a flash in the pan. Recent archaeology has established that mining was taking place in the Elenydd over 4,000 years ago. In the valley of Cwmystwyth the same people that built the cairns on the tops of Pumlumon and Drygarn Fawr turned the earth inside out in search of lead and copper. The Romans mined for gold on the Elenydd's southern margins at Dolaucothi, and subsequent generations of speculators, prospectors and adventurers sank shafts and drove adits throughout the region. The industry reached a climax in the late 19th century, when one such mine was likened to the great Potosi metal mines in Bolivia.

Pumlumon from Carn Owen (Martin Wright)

In more recent times other elements of the Elenydd's landscape have been subject to exploitation; chiefly its water. A total of eight major reservoirs have been created in the last century or so from the waters of the Pumlumon and Elenydd watersheds. Two of these, Nant y Moch (1964) and Clywedog (1967), take their waters from the northern slopes of Pumlumon, and another, Llyn Brianne (1972), captures the waters of the infant river Tywi. By far the most impressive of the Elenydd's dams and reservoirs, though, are those that form the Elan Valley system. Opened in 1904, the Elan Valley dams were built by Birmingham Corporation, and are an outstanding example of the achievements of Victorian municipal enterprise. The reservoirs they created (including the Claerwen reservoir, opened in 1952) supply Birmingham with up to 360 million litres of water a day, and without their existence one of the greatest cities in England would have long withered of thirst. The influence of the Elenydd thus extends beyond the Welsh border to the industrial heart of England.

BATTLEGROUND

Water – and the enormous condescension of dam building – is, of course, a potentially controversial subject. Pumlumon and the Elenydd are, though, no strangers to conflict. Indeed, Pumlumon is possibly most famous for the great battle that took place under in its shadow in 1401. It was at Mynydd Hyddgen, immediately to the north of Pumlumon that Owain Glyndŵr confronted and crushed the forces that had been sent to quell his famous uprising. This event, arguably the most important battle in Welsh history, initiated a brief period of national liberation that has inspired nationalists since.

Conflict is one of the key forces of history; one of the great continuities. If Pumlumon was host to one of the great battles of the Welsh past, it is also the site of one of the great battles of the present. The clash between exploitation and conservation is currently being fought over plans to turn much of the area over to massive wind farms (including one that would tower over the battleground of Hyddgen itself). Such schemes throw the history of this heartland into sharp relief. This past and future battleground is also a mirror, in which some of the cultural and environmental issues that face Wales – and humankind – are reflected. Together with the Elenydd, Pumlumon has played a massive part in the past of Wales. Without due regard to what happens there in the present, the Wales of the future will be greatly impoverished.

Further Reading:
Anthony Griffiths, *Elenydd: Ancient Heartland of the Cambrian Mountains / Hen Berfeddwlad Gymreig* (Llanrwst, Gwasg Carreg Gwalch, 2010)

12

CRADLE OF REVOLUTION – THE LOWER SWANSEA VALLEY

H. V. Bowen

The history written about the Industrial Revolution has been a very English affair. In most of the well-known textbooks Wales get barely a look in. The scene of the action is nearly always located in England. In the self-styled 'birthplace of industry' at Ironbridge Gorge and nearby Coalbrookdale; in the 'dark satanic' cotton mills of Lancashire; and in the shipyards and factories of Tyneside.

As in so much historical work on 'Britain', the perspectives offered are usually Anglocentric, and examples or evidence from Wales are usually conspicuous by their absence. As a result, there is little in the literature to help sustain any claims that Wales might have been the world's first industrial nation. And we are left with a very powerful myth which suggests that the driving forces of the all-transforming processes of industrialisation were located in England.

1750 AND ALL THAT

Of course, Welsh history has more than a few myths of its own, and one of the most enduring ones is that in Wales the coming of the Industrial Revolution was all about iron and Merthyr. Indeed, during an otherwise excellent BBC Wales television series on the history of Welsh towns, Eddie Butler told us that 'The industrial revolution in Wales began in 1750 with the iron works at Merthyr Tydfil'.

Began in 1750? With all due respect, this is nonsense! Industrialisation did not begin with a big bang, and it certainly did not begin in Merthyr. Such Mertho-centric views of the world completely ignore the vitally important contributions made by other places to modern Welsh industrialisation in earlier years. They ignore the Redbrook in the Wye valley. They ignore Neath Abbey and Aberdulais in the Neath valley. And, as usual, they ignore north-east Wales, and especially Bersham and the Greenfield Valley.

But above all such views ignore the lower Swansea valley where industrial activity of world significance was already in full swing well before a single furnace went into blast at Dowlais or Cyfarthfa.

This is not to deny the undoubted importance of Merthyr in Welsh history. Indeed, later in this book my colleague Chris Evans makes a compelling and passionate case in support of that unique iron town. And in his marvellous book on work and social conflict in early industrial Merthyr Professor Evans notes that, rightly or wrongly, Merthyr now has powerful 'totemic value' in Welsh history because of what it symbolises for working-class traditions and politics.

But if we look beyond the emergence of radical politics, and then extend that view to the period before iron and coal came to dominate Welsh industrialisation in the 19th century, the reality is that it was the copper industry that led the way. Propelling Welsh copper onto the world stage was a unique combination of natural resource, capital, labour, and entrepreneurial vision that came together in the lower Swansea valley during the first half of the 18th century.

It was the copper industry that first effectively harnessed coal technology to facilitate mass production of a high-quality metal. It was copper that led the breakout of Welsh heavy industry into world markets. It was the copper kings who created the first purpose-built workers' accommodation and townships in Britain. And it was the copper industry that created in Swansea the 'intelligent town' shaped by science, art, culture, and an insatiable thirst for all forms of new practical knowledge.

A PLACE IN WELSH HISTORY

Why the lower Swansea valley? There were of course no deposits of copper ore in the valley. But the valley possessed two critically important natural assets that acted as a magnet for the early industrialists. The sides of the valley possessed rich outcrops of easily accessible coal, while on its floor the wide river provided plenty of water and the necessary short transport link to the sea. This convinced some visionaries that it made much more financial sense to bring copper ore to the valley than it did to carry large quantities of coal to the source of that ore in the mines of Cornwall and Ireland.

The landscape of progress

As expansionist copper producers outgrew sites elsewhere in South Wales, such as Redbrook in the Wye valley, they turned their attention to Swansea as well as the Neath area, where there was already a long tradition of smelting and metal production. Leading the way were merchants from Bristol, and the first hesitant steps were taken in the lower Swansea valley when smelting houses were built at what became the Llangyfelach works at Landore in 1717. Ten years later, this works was taken on and developed by other incomers – Robert Morris from Shropshire and the influential London merchant Richard Lockwood.

Others from Bristol and London soon jumped on the bandwagon. The large White Rock works was established in the shadow of Kilvey Hill in 1737. Chauncey Townsend's lead works at Middle and Upper Bank became copper works during the 1760s and 1770s, before Matthew Boulton and his Midland partners developed the Birmingham or Ynys works from 1793 onwards. The Hafod works was built by the Cornishman John Henry Vivian in 1810, and this was followed by the Morfa works of Williams, Foster & Co. In total, 13 copper works were established by 1850.

A world-leading method of smelting soon emerged, and an array of furnaces facilitated the production of semi-refined cake as well as bars, ingots,

109

and plates. The 'Welsh method' involved multiple roastings in a long line of reverbatory furnaces, and it held sway for a century and a half after 1720.

The smelting houses were fuelled by the high-quality smokeless steam coal that was first extracted from exposed seams on Kilvey Hill, and then later from numerous pits sunk at Landore, Plasmarl, Treboeth, Cwm, Winch Wen, and Llansamlet. And, adding to the diversity, there were later spin-off industries, notably (and most dangerously) arsenic and sulphuric acid.

These interlinked industrial concerns were serviced by a transport system that was remarkable by any standards. Of course, the river Tawe remained of great importance and it soon became lined with docks, quays, and wharves. But it was its ambitiously constructed man-made transport infrastructure that enabled the valley to function so effectively.

John Smith's canal was completed in 1784 to carry coal three miles from Llansamlet to Foxhole, and a few years later Morris's Canal (later Trewyddfa Canal) connected Morriston to the river near Plasmarl.

Then, on a much grander scale, the Swansea canal was built on the western side of the valley between 1794 and 1798. It ran for over 16 miles between Abercrave and Swansea, and enabled coal to be carried to the smelting works as well as the nearby port. Some of the surviving structures, such as the aqueduct at Clydach, are of the greatest importance, and we are all deeply indebted to the Swansea Canal Society which in recent years has fought tooth and nail to protect and restore the northern stretch of the canal.

Smith's canal contained a short underground section from which coal was fed into the White Rock works. In other parts of the valley, canals were constructed to carry coal along routes beneath mountains. Most notable here was the Clyn-du underground mining canal, which was served by underground railways, and probably built by Lockwood, Morris & Co. It was constructed during the 1770s beneath Graig Trewyddfa at Morriston, and has claims to have been the world's longest canal of its type.

Coal roads, tramways and railways also made an early and important contribution to the development of the valley. Over two centuries, these functional systems were constantly upgraded and renewed, and in places such as Landore there emerged dense concentrations of interlocking transport networks.

From 1850 onward the great Landore viaduct designed by Isambard Kingdom Brunel carried the mainline railway above the valley floor and river into Swansea. It still serves its purpose today, a great reminder of the many extraordinary feats of engineering skill and vision that transformed the valley into a hotbed of industrial activity.

Other achievements put the valley at the forefront of innovation, and add to an already long list of 'world firsts'. The workers' accommodation known as Morris Castle built on a promontory overlooking the valley by Robert Morris II in the 1770s was the first such multi-storey building in Britain since Roman times.

The planned township known as Tre-Vivian (or Vivian's Town) built by the Vivian family from the 1820s onwards was the first of its type. Others followed: Morris Town (Morriston), Grenfell Town (Pentre-Chwyth), and the settlement built by Freeman & Co. at Foxhole. Each settlement had its own schools, churches, and chapel, and this gave rise to the development of cohesive communities, each with its own distinctive identity.

Of course, living conditions in the valley were blighted to a very considerable degree by sulphurous fumes and the growth of giant slag heaps. And there were strikes and disputes from time to time. But by and large the social and cultural systems built up around the smelting works were sufficiently effective to ensure avoidance of the violent confrontations between owners and workers that occurred elsewhere in Wales.

Slag heap

Nature and industry contend

Essentially places such as Merthyr and Coalbrookdale were always one-industry towns. But, over time, the industrial complex that emerged within a few square miles on the narrow floor of the valley between Llansamlet in the north and Foxhole in the south came to support the production of copper, gold, iron, lead, silver, steel, tinplate, zinc, and various alloys such as brass and spelter. Indeed, the name 'Copperopolis' does scant justice to the range of industrial activity conducted in Swansea and its immediate valley hinterland.

A survey indicates that in 1883 there were 53 works of various types within a five-mile radius of the centre of Swansea, and most of these were in the lower part of the valley. There were 36 collieries, 8 iron works, 6 tin works, 3 steel works, 6 spelter works, 12 copper works, 5 fuel works, and 13 other types of works. It is hard to think of any other place of such small size in Britain that contained a similar density and diversity of heavy industry. There was certainly nowhere else like it in Wales.

Today there are few visible physical reminders of the scope and the scale of that activity. There are no places to visit, trails to follow, or information boards to read, and in large part this helps to explain why the lower Swansea valley has been almost entirely erased from our historical consciousness. Indeed,

112

were it not for Stephen Hughes's wonderful book *Copperopolis* the details of what happened in the lower Swansea valley would have been airbrushed out of Welsh history

THE WORLD OF THE LOWER SWANSEA VALLEY

For any place to have a credible claim to be the most important place in Welsh history it is necessary for it to have had an impact beyond Wales. Its significance must be recognised from afar as well as close to home. An enduring legacy in other parts of the world only adds to the strength of any claims made on its behalf. The lower Swansea valley has certainly left a deep imprint on global history.

From the very beginning the growth of the copper concerns in the lower Swansea valley was driven by demand from international markets, and this placed it at the forefront of the processes that were shaping the emergence of a world economy. There is no escaping the fact that early interest in the valley arose from a need for Bristol merchants to manufacture the decorative copper items that were used as currency in the transatlantic slave trade. Compelling evidence for this is provided by the activities of those such as the Coster family who were involved in the early development of the White Rock works.

But the early copper industry was always about much more than slavery (and it is noteworthy that Swansea later led the way in Wales's abolition movement). An important factor in the development of Lockwood, Morris & Co. was the securing of an annual order to supply the East India Company which shipped increasing amounts of copper to Asia from 1730 onwards. The second wave of firms to establish works in the valley between 1750 and 1790 all supplied copper to the East India Company, and the combined impact of their operations was very considerable indeed. The previously favoured Japanese copper was rapidly swept from Indian and Indian Ocean markets, so much so that Swansea copper soon dominated.

A very effective export strategy began the process of yoking Asian economies to British industry. Later, during the 1830s and 1840s, the full force of imperial-industrial capitalism was to be felt in India when traditional indigenous textile industries were almost obliterated by cheap, machine-produced Lancashire cottons. But it was the smelters of the lower Swansea valley who paved the way for the successful penetration of Asia markets by British products.

This development was of seismic significance but has never been properly acknowledged by historians of Britain, let alone historians of Wales.

113

COPPER NOT COTTON

The lower Swansea valley's significance is recognised in Asia, where some scholars are well aware of the importance of Swansea for global economic development. As Ryuto Shimada has written recently, 'It was British copper, not British cotton textiles, which acted as the harbinger of the Industrial Revolution to the world economy'. As Shimada notes, nearly all of the British copper that flooded into Asian markets after 1750 was smelted in the lower Swansea valley.

But the copper industry served to integrate the global economy in other ways. Indeed, one of the most astonishing aspects of the history of the lower Swansea valley is how its entrepreneurs scoured the world after 1820 as they went in search of new supplies of copper ore. This was necessary because the mines of Cornwall, Anglesey, and Ireland became exhausted.

It meant that the smelters now derived their ore from far-flung places, not just in Europe, but in North and South America and the Antipodes. As mines in Cuba, Chile, and South Australia were connected with works in Hafod, Landore, and Morfa, the lower Swansea valley exerted a powerful influence on emerging economies across different parts of the world.

So, this essay makes the case for the lower Swansea valley being the cradle of the industrial revolution. But which industrial revolution have we been talking about? Wales's industrial revolution? Certainly. Britain's industrial revolution? Definitely. The global industrial revolution? Without a doubt. In sum, the activities centred on the lower Swansea valley served to animate the complex industrial processes that transformed the world during the 18th and 19th centuries. We are still living with the consequences today, and that is why the valley fully deserves to be regarded as the most important place in Welsh history.

Further reading:
Stephen Hughes, *Copperopolis. Landscapes of the Early Modern Industrial Period in Swansea* (2000)
For more information see www.welshcopper.org.uk

13

SUPERLATIVE AND INFERNAL GRANDEUR – MERTHYR

Chris Evans

WHERE IS WALES'S MOST HISTORIC LOCATION?

It has to be Merthyr, surely? It's been said before but it bears repeating: nowhere else has played such a pivotal role in Welsh history. Merthyr was where modern Wales began. It was where everything that had happened previously was rendered irrelevant. It may not be the most scenic location and it may not attract the most tourist footfall – one of the more misleading contemporary measures of significance – but Merthyr has profound historic substance.

MERTHYR: THE FIRST, THE BIGGEST, THE BEST...

The history of Merthyr is a history written in superlatives. It was the first town in Wales – the first real town, at least. Earlier, there had been places that had been called towns, but most of these amounted to very little: a huddle of houses in the shadow of a castle and not much more. Many places that prided themselves on their urban dignity were laughably petty. The 'towns' of pre-industrial Wales were lucky if they could scrape together 1500 inhabitants. In modern terms, they were modest housing estates, not worth a corner shop. Anyone in Wales seeking urban entertainment in the 17th or 18th centuries headed for Bristol or Shrewsbury. There was nothing at home.

Merthyr was different. The first national census in 1801 revealed that Merthyr parish had 7700 inhabitants. This was not much to boast about by later standards (or even by the standards of contemporary England) but it was enough to put everywhere else in Wales in the shade. Merthyr was rough-and-ready, of course. It was slow to acquire urban sophistication or distinguished public buildings but it was, nonetheless, the first Welsh settlement to acquire genuinely urban dimensions. It was the seat of Welsh urban modernity.

MERTHYR AND ITS RIVALS

What possible rivals might there be? Cardiff outgrew Merthyr in the second half of the 19th century and it acquired a commercial glamour with its Coal Exchange and its opulent Edwardian civic centre. All true, but in the 19th century and for much of the 20th was Cardiff anything more than a corridor between industrial Wales and the world beyond? The airs that Cardiff has given itself as a political capital and a 21st-century media hub are of recent vintage.

The furnace at Dowlais Ironworks in the 1880s

Dowlais Iron Company's Blast Furnace site under construction, c.1865

Swansea is a rival of a different sort. As an industrial settlement it can claim priority. Copper smelting began along the lower Tawe in the 1720s, some decades before iron making began in the upper Taf valley. Swansea's partisans can also point to the town's multidimensional urban character. In its 19th-century heyday Swansea was a busy international port, albeit one with a limited range of trading partners. Swansea also enjoyed its status as a resort. Swansea bay did not bear comparison with the Bay of Naples, as one over-eager 18th-century tourist was to claim, but it was a pleasing enough place at which to bathe. The success of 'Swansea by the Sea' was compromised though by the town's industrial success. Visitors had to run the reeking gauntlet of the neighbourhood's copper smelters before they could breathe in the pure sea air. Most 19th-century tourists thought better of the bargain.

Swansea has a serious claim to be the crucible of Welsh modernity but ultimately it fails the test. Its industrial history is a little too measured and its politics too humdrum. Compared with Merthyr, it is curiously passionless. But Swansea can make a plausible case for itself, at least; nowhere in North Wales can do so. An English visitor of the 1820s was emphatic on this point. The people of the North '*were half a Century behind* those of South Wales, – and *a Century behind* those of England'.

MERTHYR: IRON CAPITAL OF THE WORLD

Merthyr's importance rests four-square upon its industrial achievements. Once more we can reach for the superlatives: Merthyr was the first, or it was the biggest, or the best. Merthyr Tydfil was not the birthplace of coke smelting (we will cede that to Coalbrookdale in Shropshire) but it was where a 'coal technology package' was perfected: a system of making iron that used coal in every aspect of the production process from the blast furnaces to the forges and on to the rolling mills. This development, which constituted a decisive break with the old ways (what happened at Coalbrookdale was merely partial), began at Cyfarthfa in the 1760s. By the 1790s it had been brought to such a pitch of perfection that Merthyr parish was the most productive centre of iron making on earth. It didn't just exceed its rivals, it towered above them.

Supremacy in making iron led to spin-off achievements in engineering and transport. Richard Trevithick's revolutionary steam locomotive – a genuinely world-changing technology – had its first outing on the tram road leading south from the Penydarren ironworks. A generation later, Merthyr gave rise to Wales's first regular working railway, the Taff Vale, engineered by Isambard Kingdom Brunel himself. Girdled by tram roads and canals, stitched together with viaducts and launders, and pierced by tunnels and railway cuttings, Merthyr was the ultimate industrial environment. The noise never stopped, the smoke never ceased and, what with the furnace flare and incandescent coking heaps, night never completely fell.

Merthyr had an infernal grandeur, something to which a host of visitors testified. It was awe-inspiring. It was also deadly. Merthyr in its days of greatness was the largest concentration of Welsh people ever known, but Merthyr consumed its citizens at a shocking rate. The environment was lethal. Overcrowding, inadequate sanitation and a choking atmosphere made for an appalling mortality rate: pathogens flourished, humans did not. Those whom disease spared still had to contend with working environments that pulsed with hazard: the mines and rolling mills exacted a heavy toll, one measured in mangled limbs and premature decrepitude.

MERTHYR: PROLETARIAN POLITICS?

This was difficult to endure. How could such hardship be justified? It was a question posed with special sharpness in a town where there was such a disparity between the rewards that went to Merthyr's iron capitalists and the wages available to those who had nothing but their labour to sustain them. Inevitably, Merthyr Tydfil was a polarised town. The power of the ironmasters was stark and they relished it. Consensus was foreign to a character like

Richard Crawshay, the Yorkshireman who founded Merthyr's greatest industrial dynasty. The refusal of Crawshay and his kind to acknowledge any power other than their own had an inevitable consequence: collective resistance on the part of Merthyr's labouring population. Gwyn Alf Williams, historian extraordinaire and a son of Merthyr, identified his native town as the birthplace of the Welsh working class. The moment at which Welsh workers thrust themselves onto the historical stage came in 1831, so Williams thought, when local industrial turmoil collided with a national political crisis over the Reform Bill. The result was a local insurrection with a bloody and tragic outcome.

CHARTISM AND UTOPIA

Merthyr's political history is again the stuff of superlatives. It was home to the first workers' movement. It was where Chartism flourished and utopian schemes got a hearing. In 1868, after the Second Reform Act, it was where nonconformist Liberalism made a critical breakthrough with the election of Henry Richard as the town's MP. Later still, in 1900, Merthyr would become an early Labour stronghold by electing Keir Hardie. Small wonder, then, that Merthyr politics could be defined, in the subtitle of a book published in 1966, as 'a working-class tradition'. Today's historians might be a little shy of the sense of apostolic succession implied by that subtitle and be more ready to see contingency at work. (Hardie's election, some might argue, owed more to splits in official Liberalism than any preordained success on the part of Labour.)

Dowlais Iron Company's Number 10 and 11 furnaces under construction c.1866

Cyfartha Works, c.1902

It is a shame that more of Merthyr's extraordinary past is not visible today. There are some well-signposted landmarks still to be seen. Cyfarthfa Castle, the fantasy mansion that William Crawshay II had built in the 1820s, is still a draw. The old furnaces at Cyfarthfa are there yet – although the site is unwelcoming and visitors are left to guess at how what they can see related to an older landscape that they no longer can. Indeed, the regrettable thing about Merthyr is that so much of its globally important historic fabric has been lost (some of it relatively recently). The 'Iron Heritage Town' has seen much of that precious heritage disappear.

MERTHYR IN THE VERY LONG RUN

Be that as it may, Merthyr's importance is such that it could stand the obliteration of every visible sign of its industrial past. Indeed, it is worthwhile taking a step back to appreciate the full importance of what took place in the Taf valley two-and-a-half centuries ago. The rush of events is so rapid and so dramatic that it is hard to take in the big picture, one that transcends Wales and that will remain important 10,000 years hence, should life on our planet survive that long.

The big picture is this: there have been only two really epoch-shifting changes in the history of our species. The first was the so-called Neolithic Revolution, the first indications of which date to about 10,000 years before the present. That revolution involved the domestication of animal and plant species, which allowed our ancestors to begin the cultivation of the earth. Fixed agriculture was of fundamental significance. Hunter-gatherers had little that was certain in their lives. They were continually on the move in search of sustenance and there was no guarantee that they would find it. The growing of crops and the exploitation of animals as forms of motive power or managed stores of protein was of revolutionary import. This happened first in the Middle East and the Nile valley, then in the Yangstse valley in China, and then in the central valley of Mexico and the Andean highlands. Cultivation was hard and gruelling work but it introduced a degree of certainty into human life. When men and women produced and stored grains they eliminated starvation as a day-to-day threat. Food surpluses paved the way for more specialised and sophisticated ways of life. Once men and women could be released from the endless routine of gathering food other things were possible: occupational specialism, writing and record keeping, state structures. Most of our recorded history deals with the consequence of this: we are dealing with squabbles within or between food-rich societies.

This sort of history amounts to nothing more than variations on a theme. In the world before the Industrial Revolution there were strict limits on what was achievable. On the whole, food was grown and consumed locally. Most people remained tied to the land. Industrial processes were limited in extent because agriculture was not so productive that it could release labour to other sectors. More importantly, industry remained reliant on sources of power that were limited. Energy was most often released by burning wood, but wood was forever in short supply because every acre devoted to growing timber was an acre that could not be used for growing food.

The pre-industrial world, in other words, worked within strict limits. That meant that the possibilities of radical change were minimal. This is a world in which there may have been picturesque or dramatic incidents but not substantial social change. For so long as the world (and Wales) remained locked within the resource constraints of the pre-industrial world the comings and goings of Llywelyn-this or Owain-that really didn't matter – not in the long term. That is why what happened at Merthyr Tydfil is so vital. The transition from a wood-fired society to a coal-fuelled society – a change that happened with such force and directness in Merthyr – was an epoch-changing rupture in human affairs. It was the first important thing to happen for 10,000 years. The tapping of a subterranean energy store – coal – unleashed new possibilities for the human species, not least the possibility of limitless economic growth, the holy grail of modernity.

MERTHYR IN THE 121st CENTURY

That is why Merthyr is worth thinking about, even though its moment of world-historical centrality has long since passed. What happened at Merthyr will remain worthy of discussion after 10,000 years have passed, even after Merthyr has disappeared from the map and Wales has dwindled into a distant speck on our historical horizon. In that far distant future it is very likely that Wales will become a name that is known only to archaeologists and a handful of scholars devoted to the remote past of the human species. Experts, using whatever academic pidgin is then current, may well debate how the ancients pronounced the name of their homeland ('Way-less'? 'Wah-hulls'?). Merthyr by then will be as distant as Ur of the Chaldees is to us but that will not diminish what happened there in the second half of the 18th century.

FURTHER READING

Chris Evans, *The Labyrinth of Flames: Work and Social Conflict in Early Industrial Merthyr Tydfil* (1993)

14

A FOREIGN FIELD THAT IS FOREVER WALES – WASHBURN STREET CEMETERY

Bill Jones

It could so easily be a cemetery in Wales. 39 acres full of Welsh history, the final resting place of people who created what was once one of the most distinctive Welsh communities that has ever existed. Here rest in peace Welsh people of all ages and callings. All around are gravestones marked with familiar Welsh surnames like Davies, Edwards, Evans, Jones, Thomas and Williams. Many of the inscriptions on the stones are in Welsh. Apparently, over a hundred men and boys named John Jones and William Evans are buried here.

Here, too, are powerful reminders of the conflicts and tragedies of a turbulent Welsh industrial past. In one historic section lie the graves of 61 men and boys. They died from suffocation underground as a result of a fire in the shaft of the Avondale colliery on 6 September 1869 (the mine only had one shaft and those trapped underground had no means of escape; in all, 110 died, including two rescuers). All 61 were buried on 9 September and all the local stores and businesses were ordered to close for the day. The final cortège – 12 coffins and mourners – made its way up to the cemetery at 7 in the evening as dusk fell. The tragedy made international news, the *Western Mail* carrying several reports including lists of the deceased.

In this cemetery, too, are the graves of Benjamin Davies and Daniel Jones, two miners shot dead by soldiers on 17 May 1871 during a disturbance in a nearby street as a long coal strike reached its violent climax. Davies and Jones were buried two days later. Davies's infant son, Taliesin, had died the morning of the funeral and was buried in the same coffin as his father. A Welsh newspaper estimated that up to 10,000 people were in the cemetery attending the graveside services, which were exclusively in Welsh. Looking on were the soldiers who ringed the graveyard's boundary fence, keeping a nervous eye on the stunned and grieving Welsh community.

A GLOBAL HISTORY

But this hallowed ground isn't in Wales. It is reputedly the largest Welsh cemetery to be found anywhere in the USA, and is possibly the largest anywhere in the world outside Wales. This is the Washburn or 'Welsh' Cemetery in Hyde Park, in the city of Scranton in the north-east Pennsylvania anthracite coalfield.

CAPITAL OF THE WORLD

In the late 19th and early 20th centuries, Scranton was 'the anthracite capital of the world' and was in the top 40 largest cities in the USA. Like so many places in Wales during the same period, Scranton was the child of booming iron and coal industries. No wonder newly arrived Welsh wrote home to say that the place was exactly like Merthyr or Aberdare or Tredegar, to name but three of many obvious counterparts. Scranton, and especially Hyde Park, where the bulk of the city's Welsh lived, was also the epicentre of Welsh America during the years when Welsh migration overseas was at its greatest.

Washburn Street Cemetery, Scranton

It may seem far-fetched to suggest that Scranton's Washburn Street cemetery is the most important place in Welsh history. Probably not many of today's readers of the *Western Mail* have even heard of it, let alone been there. But this foreign field that is forever Wales needs to be remembered and treasured. It ought to be considered as one of the most important Welsh historical sites for several reasons.

First, it symbolises an often ignored important element in the history of Wales. Welsh history isn't just about the Welsh in Wales, or the Welsh in England. Large numbers of Welsh people have become parts of the histories of Argentina, Australia, Canada, New Zealand, South Africa and, of course, the USA, by far the most popular of Welsh emigrant destinations. Because of a frustrating combination of absence of statistical records and the unreliability of those that were kept, we don't know how many Welsh people in total settled overseas. Possibly as many as a quarter of a million people born in Wales were living overseas at the beginning of the 20th century.

In memory of Thomas Jones and his 14-moth-old son, Richard Isag

The Welsh have a tradition of settling overseas that goes back centuries and still continues today. In some places they settled in sufficient numbers to make a major economic and cultural impact and give those locations an unmistakeable Welsh flavour: the Chubut valley in Patagonia, the former goldfield towns of Victoria, Australia; the farming areas in Upper New York States, Wisconsin or Southern Ohio, and the coal and steel towns of Pennsylvania.

The Washburn Street cemetery represents the global history of the Welsh. It's also a fitting memorial to those ordinary Welsh people who made up the bulk of the migrants. Much of what has been written on the Welsh overseas has inevitably concentrated on those who became famous in their adoptive societies. But Welsh emigration is also a rich human tale of hopes and triumphs and failures and tragedies. The kind of stories that finally came to rest in the Washburn Street cemetery.

'THE LARGEST REAL WELSH COMMUNITY IN THE WORLD'

The Washburn Street Cemetery also deserves to figure prominently in any list of the most important places in Welsh history because it is a memorial to what was the largest and arguably the most important Welsh community outside Wales and England during the Victorian and Edwardian era. A century ago Scranton was 'a household word in Wales', as the historian David Williams described it. It was probably the most powerful magnet of all those that attracted people out of Wales during those years. In 1890 nearly 5,000 people who were born in Wales were living in Scranton. Another 5,000 were American-born children of these native Welsh. Nowhere outside England and Wales had so many Welsh inhabitants. They also formed a substantial proportion of the city's total population, forming nearly 15% of the city's diverse ethnic mix.

Scranton was also a very important cultural centre in Welsh-American life and its Welsh inhabitants took that role very seriously. In the late 19th century the city was known as 'Athen Cymry America' (the Welsh Athens of America) because of the richness of its Welsh cultural life. Some of the biggest Welsh chapels in America were located there (some of the buildings still stand). Some of the largest and most prestigious *eisteddfodau* in America were held there, including the National American Eisteddfodau of 1875, 1880, 1885, 1902, 1905 and 1908, which absorbed the attention of all of Scranton's inhabitants, whatever their nationality, and most of the Welsh in America. According to the *Western Mail*, the 1880 eisteddfod pavilion 'presented a very brilliant scene at the opening'. Several Welsh-language newspapers and magazines were published in Scranton in the 1860s, 1870s and 1880s, as were English-language ones in later decades. In the great four-day-long World's Fair International Eisteddfod held in Chicago in September 1893, the Scranton Welsh fielded not merely one but two choirs (460 choristers in all) in the Chief Choral for Mixed Voices competition. The Scranton Choral Union, led by Aberaman-born Haydn Evans, won the contest.

So strong was Scranton's Welshness during its Welsh golden era that in June 1910 the locally-published Welsh-American newspaper, the Druid, threw down a remarkable gauntlet. It demanded that the forthcoming Investiture Ceremony of the Prince of Wales, to be held in 1911, ought to take place not in Caernarfon or Cardiff but in Scranton. Scranton was the best place to host the event, it declared, because 'we are the largest real Welsh community in the world'. And when Caernarfon was chosen as the venue, the newspaper snootily riposted (in September 1910) that Caernarfon should reciprocate by sending David Lloyd George to Scranton so that he could be proclaimed as the 'uncrowned king of the Welsh people' at the following year's 'Big Welsh

Familiar Welsh surnames like Evans populate the cemetery

Day'. The Scranton Welsh would much prefer the latter to 'the investing of a dozen princes', it said. Hardly surprisingly perhaps, the Scranton Welsh community was widely regarded as being top in almost everything but bottom in modesty. And David Lloyd George did come, eventually, on a rainy evening in November 1923.

BURIED IN HIS OWN GRAVEYARD

The graveyard's official name is the Hyde Park Cemetery although it is most often known as the Washburn Street Cemetery. But for generations it has been known as the 'Welsh cemetery' or, as it appears in innumerable death notices and reports of funerals in Welsh-language Welsh American newspapers, Mynwent y Cymry or Claddfa'r Cymry. Even the Scranton city directories of the late 19th century called it the 'Welsh Cemetery'.

During its early years it was a small public burial ground for the residents of Hyde Park borough. The cemetery's first 'resident' was Margaret Lynch, who died in 1832 and who had no Welsh connections as far as I'm aware. But from the 1840s onwards, as the Welsh presence in Scranton began to grow, so too did the cemetery increasingly bear an indelible stamp of Welshness.

Fittingly, one important strand in the cemetery's history is the benevolence of a Welshman, Thomas Phillips, a leader among the Welsh and one of the

127

most generous philanthropists of his day. In 1862 the original cemetery was expanded when Phillips purchased additional land for a burial ground. At the time of his death in May 1886, the city's *Sunday Free Press* insisted that 'few men are better known or more respected in Hyde Park... To him we are indebted for the pretty Washburn Street Cemetery'.

Born in Nantyglo in 1824, Phillips emigrated to America with his parents when he was eight years old, and came to Hyde Park in 1854. A fine example of the crucial part Welsh industrial skills played in Scranton's spectacular economic development, Phillips become general manager of the Delaware, Lackawanna & Western, the largest coalmining company in the area. His life also epitomises the vibrancy of Scranton's Welsh cultural life and the impact the Welsh made in many other walks of Scranton's life. Among many things he was one of the owners and editors of the Scranton published *Baner America* (Banner of America) newspaper, a founder of the Welsh Philosophical Society, and Republican representative in the Pennsylvania State Legislature in the early 1880s. He was laid to rest on 5 May 1886, 'in his own graveyard' as a Welsh-American newspaper put it. His funeral was one of the largest that has ever taken place in West Scranton.

THE FINAL RESTING PLACE OF SCRANTON'S WELSH

Welshness burnt brightly in Scranton but relatively briefly. Eventually the Welsh language and Welsh religious and cultural institutions declined as the processes of cultural change and the adopting of new identities gathered momentum. First generation Welsh migrants passed away and subsequent generations regarded themselves far more as American than Welsh and American. And the stream of new Welsh migrants in search of a better life that had constantly replenished the city's Welshness for over half a century dried up in the inter-war years when Scranton, like Wales, experienced a savage economic depression.

In many ways, then, the Washburn Street cemetery is a striking metaphor for the rise and decline of the city's Welshness. In 1983 a Scranton resident described the cemetery as 'the final resting place of the city's Welsh'. When I spent time in Scranton in 1981 doing research for my PhD thesis on the Welsh in America, I often asked people I met 'where did all the Welsh go?' I vividly remember the answer I invariably got: 'They're in Washburn Street'.

But the history of the Washburn Street Cemetery is not just a history from below, a history that is now dead and buried. A sense of Welshness and pride in Welsh heritage still lives on in many parts of the world, as the large number of active Welsh societies overseas today shows. Scranton still has a Welsh profile through the efforts of local Welsh societies like the St David's Society of Lackawanna County and the Scranton Welsh Male Chorus.

PRESERVING FOR THE FUTURE

The Washburn Street Cemetery has itself been one of the focal points of present-day Welsh activity in Scranton. Over the years, it has had a troubled history as a result of neglect, poor maintenance and vandalism. Gravestones have been broken or have sunk into the ground and the cemetery is often used as a dumping ground. In the past 20 years local enthusiasts and organisations have worked hard to clean up the cemetery and draw attention to its historic importance because of its links with the 1869 Avondale Mine Disaster. This was the worst disaster in the history of coal mining in north-east Pennsylvania. In its aftermath the state enacted America's first mine-safety legislation.

Commemorating the 1869 Avondale mine disaster

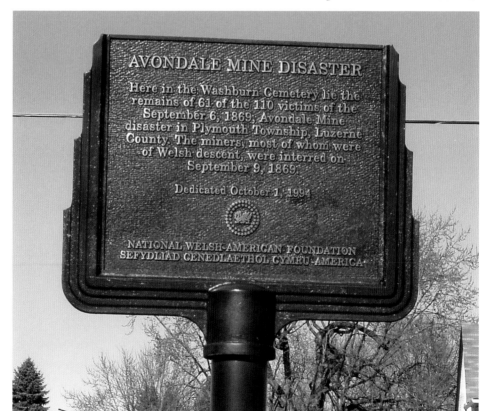

Avondale was also a very Welsh mining disaster. Sixty-nine of the 110 victims were Welsh, as were all 61 of those buried in Washburn Street Cemetery, among them William D. Jones, who left a wife and 4 children in Aberdare. In 1994 the National Welsh American Foundation, working with local groups and heritage organisations, sponsored a plaque commemorating the disaster, which was erected at the entrance to the cemetery. In 2009 a plaque was also erected adjacent to the graves. The local enthusiasts, who are determinedly striving to clean up the cemetery, repair headstones and draw attention to its historic significance, deserve support from Wales.

CONCLUSION

The Washburn Street Cemetery's 39 acres are a perfect memorial for us to remember and pay tribute to the story of Welsh people outside Wales in the 19th and early 20th centuries. This evocative field far away from Wales is not 'foreign'; it's part of the history of Wales. But it's also part of the history of America. What happens to Welshness when it is transplanted in different cultures, languages and nations is a central feature of the complex and diverse history of the Welsh people.

Finally, the Washburn Street Cemetery also lives on as a tribute to ongoing efforts all over the world to keep Welsh heritage and links with Wales alive. Perhaps Hillary Rodham Clinton, former New York Senator, former First Lady of the USA and current US Secretary of State, would agree with me. Unlike David Lloyd George nearly 70 years earlier, on 10 April 1993 she and husband Bill visited the cemetery. They were there to attend the graveside service of its most well known occupant: Hillary's father, Hugh E. Rodham, who was brought up in Scranton. His mortal remains lie alongside those of Hillary's paternal grandfather and grandmother, Hannah Jones (1882-1952), from Wales. Fittingly perhaps for a Welsh cemetery, it rained heavily on the day of the burial.

Further Reading:
William D. Jones, *Wales in America: Scranton and the Welsh, 1860–1920* (1993)

15

CUTTING A DASH – TALERDDIG

Iwan Rhys Morus

Very few people who have not travelled on the Cambrian line between Machynlleth and Newtown will have visited the Talerddig cutting. In fact, I imagine that most train travellers along that route would themselves be blissfully unaware of the fact that they had just passed through one of the most significant spots in Welsh history. There it is though, about 22 kilometres from Machynlleth heading east, and 11 kilometres or so from Caersws in the other direction. I have to confess that during my own journeys along the line I am never quite sure when I am actually passing through the cutting itself. The scrolling panoramic vision through the window of a train does not allow much of an appreciation of vertical scale, particularly close up. Vertical scale, however, is exactly what the Talerddig cutting is all about.

When the Talerddig cutting was first opened in 1862 it was, at 37 metres (120 feet), the deepest railway cutting in the world. It carved through the rugged Silurian outcrop of Talerddig for about 200 metres, carrying the Newtown and Machynlleth Railway over the highest part of its route across the Cambrian mountains, 211 metres above sea

Talerddig Cutting

level. At the time of its construction it was a huge engineering achievement. Getting across the solid, rocky spine that separated the eastern and western halves of the country had appeared a near impossible – or at least excessively expensive – undertaking. David Davies, the contractor responsible for building the twenty-odd miles of the Newtown and Machynlleth, not only succeeded, but did so far more cheaply than anyone had anticipated. But engineering achievement aside, what makes the Talerddig cutting one of the most important places in Wales? To understand that, we need to turn to railway history.

RAILWAY MANIA

The railways arrived in Wales in a fairly haphazard fashion. Particularly in the rural north and west, and along the borders, investors were wary of taking too big a risk with their money. Everyone remembered the railway craze of the 1840s and the devastating crash of 1845 that brought an end to it (the early Victorian equivalent of the dot com bubble bursting). With memories of burnt fingers lingering, investors in Welsh railway schemes during the 1850s were inclined to be a little more cautious. There was clearly money to be made building railways through Welsh hillsides, but no-one wanted to take too much of a risk in the process. The result was a patchwork of little companies, like the Mid Wales Railway and the Oswestry and Newtown, all with big ambitions but without too many miles of railway track to support them.

The key to those ambitions was to crack open the Cambrian range and push the railway through to Cardigan bay and the string of little seaside towns that lay along it. People, rather than goods, were what the little mid-Wales railways were expected to carry – and people needed places to go to. Railway promoters dreamed about transforming a place like Aberystwyth into the 'Brighton of Wales' and raking in the cash from the tourists they would bring flocking there. That was what the promoters of the Newtown and Machynlleth Railway had in mind when their company was established in 1857. Despite the name, Machynlleth was not the real destination they had in mind. Their eyes were set on Aberystwyth and the west Wales coast. That wall of solid rock at Talerddig was what lay between them and their El Dorado.

The men chosen to blaze the trail were David Davies and Thomas Savin. Both were local. Davies was born and raised in Llandinam in Montgomeryshire (as it then was). Savin was a prominent and successful merchant in Oswestry on the English borders. They had worked together before on railway projects. The two men had first become partners on the Vale of Clwyd railway during the late 1850s a few years earlier. They were experienced operators, familiar with the difficulties liable to be thrown up by the idiosyncrasies of Welsh terrain. Savin had vision as well as know-how. His was the grand plan to build a string of posh hotels along the Cambrian coast, at Aberystwyth, Borth, and points north. Passengers on the railway would buy train tickets and hotel berths together, giving Savin and his fellow shareholders a virtual monopoly on their wallets for the length of the journey.

DAVID DAVIES, VICTORIAN PARABLE

David Davies might seem the more plodding of the pair but, as it turned out, he was the one with staying power. Davies's career reads almost like a parable for Victorian self-help in the Samuel Smiles tradition – if one with a distinctively Welsh dimension. Born in 1818 he was the son of a tenant farmer who had only recently moved to Montgomeryshire from Cardiganshire. He did not stay long at school (which cost his family a weekly sixpence). By the time he was seventeen he was supplementing the meagre family income to the tune of as much as a pound a day by sawing timber for local farmers. By 1844 the Davies clan were prosperous enough to move to a far larger 150-acre farm higher up the Severn valley. Two years later the father died, leaving David Davies as head of the family.

By 1850, Davies was working for the county surveyor as a contractor, building roads and bridges. The move from roads to railways seemed a natural one. In 1855 the Llanidloes and Newtown Railway Company advertised for tenders to build the first section of track. A local man who knew the terrain intimately, Davies submitted the lowest tender and got the job. He was soon in charge of building the entire line. When work on the line stopped in 1858 due to financial difficulties, Davies turned his attention to the Vale of Clwyd and partnership with Savin. By 1859 the partners were back at work on the Llanidloes and Newtown, having cannily agreed payment in unissued shares rather than cash. When the time came to find contractors to carry the railroads westwards, the canny duo seemed the obvious choice.

This was where Thomas Savin's grand plan for railways and hotels along the Cardigan bay coast was to come into play. The plan was not just to push the railways over the rocky central spine of Wales but to build northward from Aberystwyth as well. The tracks would join at Glandyfi and head up the North Wales coast for Pwllheli and the Llŷn peninsula. Savin dreamed of a Welsh Riviera. The key to it all would be Talerddig. To make their own and the shareholders' fortunes they needed to cross the mountains. Without that breakthrough the coastal line would be a train journey to nowhere. But this was also where the partnership between Davis and Savin would come to a sticky end. Davies did not trust his partner's vision. They split the undertaking between them. Savin took the coastal line and the hotels. Davies took on the arduous business of getting the railway through Talerddig's solid rock to Machynlleth.

ROAD TO THE SEA

Savin started laying track and building hotels with astonishing speed. The Castle Hotel in Aberystwyth went up so quickly the architect barely had time to produce plans for the builders. It cost £80,000 and opened in 1865. Davies, on the other hand, had to decide what to do about Talerddig. Getting there was relatively straightforward. Getting through the rock was a different matter. Davies doubtless pondered the problem as his workers pushed the line westward. The original plans called for a tunnel bored through half a mile of rock. Davies had a better idea. He would carve a cutting through the rock instead. This had two big advantages. It would make the rails easier to maintain. And it would provide him with a cheap source of building material for the embankments and bridges he would need to carry the line back down towards Machynlleth and the sea.

The biggest problem at Talerddig, as it turned out, was not stone but water. The rock was surrounded on three sides by boggy ground. To drain the bog, Davies diverted the river Carno so that it flowed westwards into the Dyfi instead of eastwards into the Severn at Caersws. The cutting itself repeatedly flooded as the workers tapped underground springs. It took two years for Davies and his men to carve their way through Talerddig with sweat and gunpowder. The decision to cut rather than tunnel proved inspired, though. With plenty of building stone at his disposal Davies could now move steadily down the Dyfi valley. He had set himself a tight deadline. He had promised the investors that the line would reach Machynlleth by 1 May 1862, the day the International Exhibition opened in London.

David Davies kept his promise. The train left Caersws at three o'clock in the afternoon on 1 May 1862. At Talerddig it stopped to pick up some wagon loads of stone to test the weight bearing capacity of the bridges on the way down. David Davies himself took the controls at Comins Coch. When the train and its triumphant driver reached Machynlleth they were welcomed with 'a perfect Babel of sounds, Welsh, English, cannons, music, huzzas and everything'. The actual opening ceremony did not take place until 3 January the following year. Davies presented Lady Vane with a silver spade in commemoration. Later, at his own private ceremony, he gave his workmen a hearty meal and distributed £500 between them. The ceremony even attracted a lengthy notice in the *Illustrated London News* a few weeks later, with two engravings – one of the ceremony itself and the other of the magnificent Talerddig cutting.

The Talerddig cutting certainly made David Davies's career. It was an outstanding engineering feat, comparable with anything achieved by the great engineers of the Great Western or the London and Birmingham who were his near contemporaries. Davies certainly understood what an important place Talerddig was for him. According to his biographers, standing above the cutting after its completion, he declared: 'I often feared this was going to be the rock of my destruction, but with hard work and Heaven's blessings it has proved to be the rock of my salvation'. There were rumours that this was almost too true. There had been plenty of good building stone from the cutting left after finishing the railway. Davies sold it and the proceeds formed the foundation of the fortune he later made in the South Wales coalfields.

INDUSTRIAL EDUCATION

Davies went on from Talerddig cutting to become one of Wales's greatest industrial entrepreneurs of the second half of the 19th century. He built more railways, including the ambitiously named Manchester and Milford – which went nowhere near either place. The main arena for his future exploits was to be industrial South Wales, however. By the end of the 1860s he had branched out into coal. Davies and the Ocean Colliery Company he had established turned the Rhondda into one of the world's major centres of coal production by the end of the 19th century. Davies's clashes with the Bute family who controlled the Taff Vale Railway and Cardiff Docks led to yet another enterprise. Davies built Barry Docks to get around the Bute stranglehold and turned Barry into the biggest coal exporting port in the world.

So as we try to understand the important place of Talerddig cutting in Welsh history we have to recognize David Davies himself as one of its most important legacies. Talerddig made Davies as much as Davies made the cutting. It made his name and reputation as one of the great railway engineers. Davies's success at Talerddig transformed him from a local to a national operator. It expanded his horizons. In fact his next railway contract after Talerddig was in Sardinia. It also provided the foundation for his future fortune. Without Talerddig there would have been no Rhondda and no Barry Docks (and therefore no *Gavin and Stacey*). Wales would have looked a very different place.

As much as Davies's success, much of Talerddig cutting's significance for Wales lies in his partner Thomas Savin's failure too. Within three years of the cutting's completion, Savin, who had abandoned Talerddig to Davies, was bankrupt. The plan to build luxury hotels along the Welsh Riviera had proved a fiasco, as Davies had predicted. But despite Savin's failure, tourists did come through Talerddig cutting in significant numbers and transformed the economy of Cardigan Bay and its little towns in the process. By the beginning of the 20th century, the Cambrian Railway, successor of the myriad little local railway companies of which the Newtown and Machynlleth had been one, was advertising Aberystwyth as the 'Biarritz of Wales' after all. The transformation of towns like Aberystwyth, Barmouth and Tywyn into seaside holiday towns was a direct consequence of the existence of Talerddig cutting.

THE UNIVERSITY OF TALERDDIG

In Aberystwyth's case there was another consequence – both of Savin's failure and of Davies's success. The ill-fated Castle Hotel was sold in 1867 for a mere £10,000 to the promoters of a new institution – what would in 1872 become the University College of Wales. Davies, of course, would be one of the new university college's most assiduous supporters. The College by the Sea and the University of Wales that grew out of it was Wales's first distinctively national institution. It was established in the face of government indifference and with money largely raised in Wales. It would probably be going a little too far to say that without Talerddig there would have been no University of Wales. It would certainly have had a different history though and probably would not have been in Aberystwyth.

The most important thing about Talerddig cutting, however, is that it reminds us of something that we in Wales tend to forget rather too often. We all know, of course, that Wales has an industrial past. But we tend to think of it as something that came from the outside – something that 'they' did to 'us'. Talerddig should remind us that it was often no such thing. Talerddig shows us that much of Wales's Victorian industry was made in Wales. Talerddig cutting

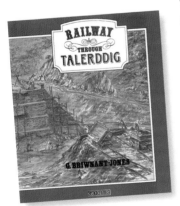

was carved through the rocky spine of Wales by Welsh ingenuity and know-how – and Welsh muscle. Talerddig shows us that technological enterprise is not something alien to Welsh culture. It is as much part of who and what we are as chapel, *eisteddfodau* or rugby. That is why Talerddig is such an important place.

Further Reading
C. P. Gasquoine, *The Story of the Cambrian: A Biography of a Railway* (Llandybie, 1973)

136

16

ANCIENT AND MODERN – CARDIFF CASTLE

Andrew Richardson

On 10 September 1947, the Fifth Marquess of Bute handed over the keys of Cardiff castle to the Lord Mayor, Alderman George Ferguson, presenting it with its parkland to the people of Cardiff. After receiving thanks for what the mayor considered 'a gesture of truly royal nature', Lord Bute replied that 'naturally he had certain regrets, but he felt great satisfaction in handing to the city the castle from which it sprang'. This sentiment was reflected in the words of the *South Wales Echo* at the time, which observed that it was 'no longer Cardiff Castle, but *Cardiff's* Castle'.

As the centuries-old Bute standard was lowered from the Norman keep and replaced with the city flag, press commentators devoted many column inches to the history of the castle as a monument of Cardiff's antiquity. There is an unquestionable interdependence between the development of the castle and city. This symbiosis is not limited to the physical evolution of the city's urban landscape, but also the development of civic consciousness and identity. Cardiff Castle is an important symbol of the city's economic prosperity, cultural sophistication, administrative power and historical memory. Without this iconic building and the events that took place both within its walls and beyond, Cardiff would not be the capital city of Wales today.

THE *CAER* ON THE TAF

Cardiff Castle is steeped in over 2,000 years of history. Built c AD55, the Roman fort or *castrum* was part of a system of frontier posts from a legion based at Caerleon, founded by the Roman General Julius Frontinus upon his conquest of the Silures, a powerful and warlike tribe of ancient Britain who occupied South Wales. From this settlement a civil community grew. It is from this period that the name Cardiff (*Caerdydd*) is derived, from the Welsh *Caer*, a castle or fort, and *Taf*, the river – the 'Castle on the Taf'.

Abandoned by the retreating Romans, the castle fell into disrepair. Centuries later, following the collapse of several feudal lordships in Glamorgan, it was taken during the Norman Conquest in 1091. Sir Robert Fitzhamon, Earl of Gloucester, found use for the crumbling Roman walls as the foundations to house his Norman garrison. First erecting a fortified keep on a 40-feet-high artificial mound, the Normans cut a deep moat and threw the soil onto the walls to create a formidable defensive bank. Towers and apartments were later built by Gilbert De Clare in the 13th century and stone walls were erected around the town, to meet the opposition of the powerful Llywelyn, Prince of Wales. Despite this substantial fortification the castle and town were later taken by Owain Glyndŵr and his forces in 1404, decimating the town for decades.

The castle was remodelled as a residence in the 15th century by Richard Beauchamp, Earl of Warwick in 1430. From this point, the castle and its borough became the seat of great noblemen. It was the nucleus of the local community, with daily town life regulated by the authority of the medieval lord. Within the castle walls, solemn court proceedings were held, trading regulated and taxes collected. Cardiff was now a market town, with amenities including a hospital, hotels and churches. A colourful municipal calendar consisting of fairs, hunts and tournaments maintained the focus of the community on the castle.

A 'NOBLE' HOME

The Herbert family acquired the castle and Glamorganshire in the 16th century. Following the upheaval of the Civil War, in which the castle was occupied by a royalist garrison, what remained of the Herbert estates passed through marriage to Thomas,1st Viscount Windsor on his marriage to the daughter of the 7th Earl of Pembroke in 1703. The estate was conveyed again in 1766 to another family through the marriage of the heiress, Charlotte Jane Windsor, to John Stuart. He was created Baron Cardiff in 1776 and twenty years later, Marquess of Bute.

Of unquestionable aristocratic pedigree, the Stuarts of Bute were directly descended from King Robert II of Scotland. These Scottish nobles brought industry, prosperity and dynamic growth to Cardiff by harvesting the 'black gold' of the South Wales Coalfield and facilitating its global export. Intensive industrialisation swelled the population of Cardiff a hundredfold, from 1,870 in

1801 to 182,000 in 1911, a by-product of the burgeoning industries that made Cardiff a thriving epicentre. Such prosperity and growth was accompanied by growing civic confidence and prominence. Cardiff was heralded as one of the most successful examples of the industrial revolution with contemporaries declaring it the 'Chicago of Wales' and the 'Coal Metropolis of the World'.

THE CREATOR OF MODERN CARDIFF

Accredited as the 'creator' of Modern Cardiff, John Stuart, the Second Marquess of Bute was the epitome of the aristocratic industrialist and landowner. Imbued with a strong sense of duty, philanthropy and a tireless work ethic, Bute was widely recognised as an innovative estate manager, shrewd entrepreneur and dock builder. When he inherited, the estate was in a 'seriously neglected condition' and required enormous investment. Bute completed the West Dock in 1839, transporting 350,000 tonnes of iron and coal from the Rhondda valley to the docks in the first year alone. From the castle, Bute ran his estate with his powerful chief agent, Edward Priest Richards, also the town's bailiff and mayor. On the night of his death in March 1848, he expressed the hope that his successor would live to see the commercial seaport become a 'second Liverpool'.

The Marquess of Bute   The Marchioness of Bute

THE THIRD MARQUESS OF BUTE

In 1849 the widowed Marchioness wrote to Richards: 'The whole fabric of our affairs has been shivered to the foundations by Lord Bute's death'. Bute left a six-month-old heir, John Patrick Crichton Stuart and an intimidating legacy. With the estate held in trust until his majority in 1868, Bute received considerable media attention due to his immense wealth and controversial Catholic conversion. For many, Bute was to prove a disappointment; a reclusive, taciturn and unassuming scholar, he failed to live up to the expectations thrust upon him from birth. 'Lord Bute was not an ideal nobleman', recalled the *Western Mail* in 1900, 'He was too fond of ease, too retiring and too modest. He can hardly be said to have risen to his great opportunities and vast responsibilities'.

Bute was dismissed by contemporaries and historians alike as the self-indulgent beneficiary of great wealth, unable to escape his father's shadow. When the Third Marquess died his *Western Mail* obituary was headlined 'Death of the son of the Creator of Cardiff'. Bute had little interest in politics and estate administration, preferring to contribute to society through philanthropy; providing monetary benefactions and patronage to the arts, higher education, hospitals and establishing civic institutions and peoples' parks. He also founded the *Western Mail* in 1869. Despite his aversion to public appearances, Bute inherited the paternalistic *noblesse oblige* of his father and the desire to develop, design and build. It was the latter that was to provide his most enduring legacy.

LORD OF BRICKS AND MORTAR

Bute once wrote 'My luxury is art. I have considerable taste for art and archaeology, and happily the means to indulge them'. The combination of his intellectualism, architectural interests and medievalism led Bute to prefer living in the past than the present. This was expressed in his splendid restoration of Cardiff Castle in partnership with the 'soul-inspiring' William Burges. The medieval recreation of the gothic castle was closely connected to the need to announce that the castle was once again the seat of a powerful nobleman.

THE AESTHETICS OF POWER

In his survey, Burges noted that 'we must never lose sight of the fact that Cardiff Castle is not an antiquarian ruin but the seat of the Marquess of Bute'. The new building was intended as an assertive and durable display of power. The development of a domineering middle-class had eroded aristocratic control, disrupted the social order and challenged ancient notions of hereditary privilege and authority. In response the aristocracy adapted, ceding 'real' political power and exchanging it for 'unreal prestige'. Bute was able to capitalise upon the middle-class thirst for civic pageantry and the beautification of the urban environment. The castle was to become emblematic of this new aristocratic civic role and serve as a 'legitimising symbol of antiquity'.

The medieval-inspired interior of the castle, with its eclectic mixture of decoration styles, affords the visitor with overwhelming splendour, intricate sculptures, colourful religious iconography, fantastic murals and vaulted ceilings trimmed with gilded carvings. Welsh legend and history also had a place, as the sumptuous banqueting hall murals depict the life

Cardiff Castle, c.1870s

of the Norman Lord of Glamorgan, Robert the Consul. The ambitious project provided Bute and Burges with the opportunity to translate their imaginations into wonderful realities and push architectural boundaries. As Burges wrote in 1871, 'Mere convenience and good construction are not the only requisites in such a building. The sculptor and the painter must be called in to make the brute stones and plastered walls speak and tell a story'. The rooms, grand staircases, ceilings and halls are a romantic reflection of medieval Gothic revivalism and the stately edifice provided a spectacular silhouette that demanded the attention of the Victorian observer.

Outside, the centrality of the castle was emphasised through the manipulation of the townscape, creating plentiful space to allow passers-by to admire the venerable structure which 'seized the horizon.' This was accentuated by the impressive clock tower. The four-dial 'zodiac' clock is stamped with the heraldic shields and coronets of the Bute family and crowned with a copper flag pierced with the Stuart lion. The tower was a visual representation of power – it was the highest structure in Cardiff.

141

BUTE AND THE BEASTS

On the ground, the castle boundary wall afforded Cardiff citizens with an aesthetic novelty – an array of carefully sculpted animals that included lions, apes, a bear and a hyena. Reportedly, when the animals were completed, Lord Bute returned home from an overseas trip and ordered the animals be taken down and re-carved because he thought their expressions were not ferocious enough! The picturesque pre-Raphaelite moat garden was designed for public use and on Sundays the grounds were opened to the public for people to stroll, picnic and socialise.

THE GOLDEN AGE OF CIVIC GRANDEUR

It was this communal use of the castle that allowed it to function as a 'municipal' building. The castle became the venue for festivals, celebrations and exhibitions. Bute family birthdays, weddings and anniversaries were public events in the town. The Third Marquess's 1868 coming-of age celebrations were said to be 'Cardiff's first truly civic event', marked by four days of pomp and ceremony; concerts, regattas, feasts, fireworks and a procession from the docks to the castle through lavishly decked and crowded streets. Similar scenes occurred on the occasion of his marriage to Gwendolen Howard in 1872 and the couple's silver wedding anniversary in 1897, which was, the *Western Mail* declared, 'the greatest social function ever held in Cardiff'. This was indicative of Cardiff's civic consolidation, which sought to integrate urban society around a Bute-focused celebratory framework.

Cardiff Castle, c.1910

The Lord Mayor of Cardiff - "Hywel Dda."	Viscount Tredegar - "Owen Glyndwr."
Lady Bute - - "Dame Wales."	Lord Mostyn "His Ancestor at Bosworth."
Lady Llangattock -	The Archdruid of Wales "The Archdruid."
"Wife of Owen Glyndwr."	The Chief Constable of Glamorgan
Lady Ninian Stuart - "Glamorgan."	"Chief Ruffian."

REALISTIC ONSLAUGHT ON CARDIFF CASTLE

BY HUNDREDS OF EMINENT FOOTBALLERS.

MAGNIFICENT FIREWORK DISPLAYS

JULY 28th and 29th, by BROCK, of the Crystal Palace.

BAND OF THE ROYAL MARINES

Nothing like this Pageant has ever been seen in the Principality before.

PERFORMANCES:

JULY 26 to 31 at 2.30 p.m. AUGUST 2 to 7 at 7.30 p.m.

Two Performances on Saturday, July 31st and August 7th, and Bank Holiday 2.30 and 7.30.

THE EVENING PERFORMANCES WILL BE BRILLIANTLY ILLUMINATED BY 10,000 MOST POWERFUL ELECTRIC LAMPS, MAKING THE SCENE A PERFECT FAIRYLAND.

ADMISSION · 1/-

(STANDING ACCOMMODATION ONLY).

RESERVED SEATS :---10/6, 7/6, 5/- and 2/6

Booking Office---PAGEANT HOUSE, Wharton Street, CARDIFF.

Poster advertising the National Pageant of Wales, 1909

HOST AND DEFENDER

The Butes were no strangers to playing host. Societal dinners, balls and functions were regularly held at the castle for the town elite, and open days, feasts and public oxen roasts for townspeople. The Roman Catholic Corpus Christi festival was held annually at the castle from 1874. Bute also used the castle during the 1883 National Eisteddfod at Cardiff, holding a grand concert of Welsh music complete with triple harps. An ardent Welshman, Bute made keynote speeches at several eisteddfodau, and remained a staunch defender of the language and its culture.

A 'MODEL MAYOR'

Lord Bute was elected Mayor of Cardiff in 1890–91. He was the first peer in Great Britain to be elected to municipal office since 1727. Only made possible by his political impotence, it was an important social step that endorsed the supremacy of middle-class values with the Marquess as the 'figurehead' of an increasingly gentrified, civic elite.

As the mayoral residence, the castle became an extension of the town hall. The Marquess and Marchioness hosted important guests of the town, visiting associations and societies, royal visitors and public events. The Council used Bute's tenure of office to its full potential, proudly 'showing off' their noble civic leader.

THE METROPOLIS OF WALES

In 1897, Lord Bute sold Cathays Park to the Corporation of Cardiff for £150,000. The Portland-stone City Hall, Law Courts and University College were completed in the early 20th century, with Cardiff awarded city status in 1905, and the successful bid for the National Museum quickly following. The location, design and structure of the civic centre had symbolic meaning; it lies adjacent to the castle, and architects ensured that the collegiate, democratic, white-toned architecture sharply contrasted with the feudality of the castle. Pointedly, the clock tower on city hall is higher than the castle's, symbolically made so by the dragon perching on the dome. Together, the castle and the civic centre were key elements in the conversion of civic identity into national aspiration. With a collection of strong civic and national institutions, Cardiff assumed leadership of the nation, becoming Capital of Wales in 1955. As former First Minister Rhodri Morgan noted, '[Bute] didn't make Cardiff the Capital of Wales, but it could never have become the capital without Bute'.

THE CASTLE TODAY

The gift of the castle to the people of Cardiff in 1947 was a philanthropic act with a very real impact. The castle's diverse historic past unified civic identity and ensured its transfer to Welsh national identity. The castle remains a dynamic, forward-looking institution, currently undergoing an £8 million conservation programme. As it has throughout the centuries, it continues to host a myriad of events; weddings, festivals, concerts, jousts and royal visits. It is home to the Royal Welsh's Regimental Museum and provides thousands of school pupils with an engaging educational programme. It is also a hugely popular tourist attraction which welcomes over 250,000 people every year. In short, it is the heart around which the arteries of the city flow.

Yet just as important as the building were the people who lived there. It has been the fort of a Roman general, a stronghold for a conquering Norman knight, the administrative centre for medieval lords and an opulent home for industrious noblemen. Their names are used every day – Herbert, Fitzhamon, Bute, Dumfries, Windsor and Mountstuart – permanently grafted onto modern Cardiff in parks, streets, crescents and squares. Busy Cardiff citizens occasionally glance up at their bronze statues, walk around their buildings and pass their monuments, yet rarely stop to consider the people behind the architecture which defines the urban environment. For modern Cardiff, the most important castle residents were the Butes, who catapulted Cardiff into the Industrial Revolution and helped to consolidate an enduring historical legacy. The castle is an essential part of civic and national identity, originally manifested through a Bute-sponsored civic culture. Cardiff Castle remains the permanent connection to the Capital of Wales's past, present and future, a jewel in the crown of the city which sprang from it.

Further Reading
John Davies, *Cardiff and the Marquesses of Bute* (1980)

17

SUPER PIT AND SLAUGHTERHOUSE – PENALLTA COLLIERY

Ben Curtis

WHY PENALLTA COLLIERY?

Penallta colliery, located near Ystrad Mynach in the Rhymney Valley, might seem at first glance an odd choice as a candidate for the most important building in Welsh history. Closed for over twenty years now, its pithead winding gear rusty and silent, the colliery buildings today sit perched on the edge of a brand new housing estate that has spread slowly but surely over much of the surrounding colliery surface. My selection of Penallta colliery is not so much for what it is nowadays but what it represents in terms of the history of the region's famous coalfield. Although born and brought up in the Rhymney Valley, I aim to demonstrate in this essay that there is more to my choice than simply local bias! In order to understand why this is important, though, we need to get a better sense of the immense significance of the coal industry in shaping modern South Wales.

THE COAL INDUSTRY AND THE CREATION OF MODERN SOUTH WALES

South Wales is built on coal, both geologically and historically. It is not an exaggeration to say that the coal industry was the main reason behind the creation of much of modern South Wales. With the exception of Merthyr Tydfil and the other 'iron towns' of the Heads of the Valleys, most of the towns and villages of the South Wales coalfield owe their existence to the explosive growth of the coal industry in the 19th and early 20th centuries. The most dramatic example of this was provided by the Rhondda valleys, which by the

1870s had become the coalfield's main coal-producing district. This meteoric economic development was made possible by a truly astonishing rate of inward migration. In 1851 there were only 951 residents in the Rhondda; this figure had climbed to 55,000 by 1881 and reached an eventual peak of 167,000 in 1924. By this time there were more people living in the Rhondda than in Cardiganshire, Merionethshire and Montgomeryshire combined. In addition to this, the coastal towns of Cardiff, Barry, Newport and (to a lesser extent) Swansea owe much of their modern-day size and status to the wealth that they accrued from the coal trade.

Looking back from the early years of the 21st century, it seems difficult to imagine now just how absolutely central the coal industry was to the shaping of modern South Wales. The early 20th century saw the zenith of the coalfield's economic power, with its peak production figure of 57 million tonnes being reached in 1913. By this time, there were over 234,000 miners and hundreds of pits in South Wales. South Wales was the largest coalfield in Britain, supplying 19.7% of the British coal output and almost one-third of the entire world exports of coal of all types. In 1913, Barry and Cardiff were the two biggest coal-exporting ports in the world. Equally significant – and not

Raising the NCB flag at Penallta in 1947

Penallta Colliery, 1966

unrelated to this – was the growth of bitter industrial conflict, marked by major strikes and the spread of radical left-wing ideas amongst the South Wales miners. Taken together, these factors made the South Wales coalfield a key potential flashpoint for British domestic politics at the time.

The coal miners were central to the shaping of the economics, politics and society of South Wales during the 20th century. The South Wales Miners' Federation (and its successor, the NUM South Wales Area) was much more than a union, in many respects. In addition to representing its members, it played a broader role within coalfield society. Its Workmen's Institutes spread throughout the Valleys, ran leisure and cultural events, established medical schemes and built libraries for their members. Although coal's importance diminished as the 20th century progressed, the South Wales miners and their industry remained an important part of the society and economy of Wales through until the 1980s.

The modern history and identity of the Valleys is still strongly influenced by its mining past, despite the physical disappearance of most of the collieries. (Penallta RFC are known as 'the Pitmen', for example.) On one level this is due to continued external perceptions of South Wales as being synonymous with coal, a factor which is consciously reinforced by such tourist attractions as the Rhondda Heritage Park and the Big Pit Mining Museum. In a more subtle and pervasive way, too, coal mining – specifically, coal-mining trade unionism – has been a formative influence on the 'labourist' mental outlook of the Valleys, characterised by close-knit, working-class communities and – generally – voting for the Labour Party. For more than a century, the history of the South Wales coal miners and their industry, whether for better or worse, was central to shaping contemporary Wales.

148

THE SIGNIFICANCE OF PENALLTA COLLIERY WITHIN THE SOUTH WALES COALFIELD

Of all the mining valleys of South Wales, the ones most commonly associated with coal in the popular imagination are the Rhondda valleys. Nevertheless, it is worth remembering that the general phenomena of booming coal output and rapid population growth that made the Rhondda famous also applied to the rest of the coalfield. Consequently, I would like to suggest that Penallta could be considered as the single most important colliery in South Wales – not just in terms of the place itself, but also what it represented. At its peak in the early 20th century, Penallta was one of the largest and most important pits in South Wales, employing 3,208 men in 1931. The colliery was established during 1906–09 and was one of the high-tech 'super pits' of its day. The interwar years saw Penallta consolidate its position. It was one of the most productive pits in Britain, producing over 3,000 tonnes of coal a day

THE SHOWCASE PIT

Penallta was built by the Powell Duffryn Steam Coal Company, the largest coal mining company in both South Wales and Britain. At its peak, the company owned over seventy collieries in South Wales and accounted for about one-third of the coalfield's output. Penallta was the jewel in the crown for Powell Duffryn, a status it retained right up until the nationalisation of the coal industry in 1947. Penallta was consistently one of the company's most profitable pits during the interwar years: alongside Britannia and Bargoed collieries, also in the Rhymney valley, it played a key role in underpinning the company's performance through its low-cost production of vast amounts of high quality steam coal. Located a short distance away from the company's headquarters in Tredomen, Ystrad Mynach, Penallta was Powell Duffryn's showcase pit, intended to be one of the best and most modern collieries to be found anywhere in Europe.

and regularly breaking national and European output records at this time. Its maximum production figure was reached in 1930, when 2,808 men produced 975,603 tonnes of saleable coal.

'THE SLAUGHTERHOUSE' AND 'POVERTY AND DOLE'

Penallta's status as the star performer of the biggest coalowning company in Britain did not necessarily confer any favoured status on the miners who worked there, however – in many respects exactly the opposite was the case. Powell Duffryn had a reputation amongst the South Wales miners as a particularly poor employer, in terms of pay, conditions and workplace safety. Powell Duffryn was also one of the bitterest opponents of the miners' union, the South Wales Miners' Federation (SWMF, better known simply as 'the Fed'). It was a grim joke amongst its workforce that the 'PD' written on the company's coal wagons did not stand for 'Powell Duffryn' but 'Poverty and Dole' instead!

Another characteristic feature of working conditions in the South Wales coal industry was the high incidence of accidents and disasters. These could range from relatively minor injuries to individuals to major tragedies that devastated entire communities. The worst mining disaster in British history occurred in 1913, when 439 miners died in a colliery explosion at Senghennydd in the Rhymney valley. Such disasters served to further inflame an already embittered mining community, since the coalowners' cavalier attitude towards safety regulations was held to be the main cause of the accidents. Even though Penallta was not the scene of a major disaster on this scale, the conditions underground were a cause for great concern both for its workers and for the SWMF. An investigation by the 'Fed' in the 1930s led to a damning report on the conditions and workplace safety in the Powell Duffryn collieries.

THE SLAUGHTERHOUSE

Not for nothing was Penallta known amongst miners as 'the slaughterhouse'. This image of Penallta was so deeply ingrained that in certain respects it even persisted after the industry had been nationalised in 1947. One mineworker who transferred to Penallta in the 1960s later recalled his reluctance to do so, due to the pit's historically poor safety record: 'Penallta in the Twenties had a bad reputation; it was regarded as a death pit. There were more accidents in Penallta than any other pit'.

PENALLTA UNDER NATIONALISATION

As the 20th century progressed, a serious problem for the South Wales coalfield was the relatively low level of technology in its pits, compared to those of other British coalfields. Penallta was the first colliery in South Wales to install a fully mechanised coalface, when a Meco Moore coal-cutting machine was introduced there in 1945. This was one of the first power-loading machines to be adopted by a British colliery, machines that both cut the coal and loaded it onto a conveyor for transportation out of the pit. Various geological and technological problems meant that the rest of the coalfield was slow to follow Penallta's lead in this respect. Only 6% of South Wales coal output was cut mechanically in 1955, a figure which had risen to 36% by 1961. The 1960s saw this process continue and by 1970 mechanisation had increased to 80%.

One of the dominant features of this history of the South Wales coalfield in the 1960s was a sweeping programme of colliery closures, as the National Coal Board (NCB) attempted to make the industry a smaller but more efficient coal

The ravages of industry at Penallta in 1970

producer. 86 collieries closed in South Wales between 1959 and 1970 and in the late 1960s Penallta was one of the pits that was officially classified as being at risk. Here, though, the miners used unorthodox strategies to avoid closure, running a waste minimisation campaign and even hiring a public relations firm to help them to argue their case. The story attracted the attention of the national press and the consequent boost to morale at the pit helped to raise production sufficiently to escape closure. By June 1969, Penallta had been saved.

Although not regarded as particularly militant or politically radical by the general standards of the South Wales NUM, the Penallta lodge nevertheless participated fully in the national miners' strikes of the 20th century, in 1926, 1972, 1974 and 1984–85. During the last of these, Penallta was involved with two events in particular which highlighted the seriousness of the issues at stake. In April 1984, one miner died in an accident while carrying out safety work at the pit, whilst two others were killed in September 1984 on picket duty outside Llanwern steelworks. Despite all the hardships that the miners and their families faced, only a small handful of strikebreakers went back to work at Penallta during the entire dispute. In March 1985, once the strike was over, the Penallta miners marched back to their colliery behind their lodge banner. This loyalty to their union was characteristic of the mining communities of South Wales.

About one-third of the remaining collieries in South Wales were closed within a year of the end of the strike in 1985, with most of the rest following shortly afterwards. Penallta was one of the few pits in the coalfield that was chosen to undergo a programme of modernisation, with £3.5 million being invested in rapid coal-winding skips and a new heavy-duty high-technology coalface. By March 1991, the colliery was producing 590,000 tonnes per annum of saleable coal, its highest-ever per-capita productivity rate. Despite this, it was unable to escape the broader crisis facing the industry. Penallta finally closed in November 1991, a casualty of the mass pit closures that preceded the privatisation of British Coal in 1994 and the return of the coal industry to the private sector.

PENALLTA LEADERS

Penallta colliery produced several noteworthy individuals who attained prominence within the SWMF and the NUM South Wales Area. The best known of these was Ness Edwards. Following his early career as a miner and miners' leader, Edwards became the Labour MP for Caerphilly from 1939 to 1968, and attained the role of Postmaster General during the Attlee government of 1950–51. He was also a pioneer in the field of modern labour history in Wales. His main books were *The Industrial Revolution in South Wales* (1924), *The History of the South Wales Miners* (1926) and the *History of the South Wales Miners' Federation, Vol. I* (1938), as well as writing about the Chartist movement in South Wales. An important development in Edwards's career occurred in September 1927 when he was appointed as the full-time secretary of the SWMF lodge at Penallta colliery. In the aftermath of the miners' defeat following the General Strike of 1926, the lodge there was in a much weakened position and Edwards worked diligently to rebuild 'Fed' membership at the colliery. Having won a good reputation at Penallta, Ness was appointed as the SWMF miners' agent for East Glamorgan in 1932. It was in his role as miners' agent that Edwards was to play a key role in one of the most important events of the 1930s in the coalfield: the defeat of the rival 'company union' and the re-establishment of the 'Fed' as the trade union of the South Wales miners. Charlie Blewett was the Penallta lodge secretary in the 1960s and 1970s and was a respected figure within the South Wales NUM, who also stood as the unsuccessful Labour candidate for Cardiff North West in the 1974 general election. In addition to these, shortly before the closure of the colliery in 1991, Penallta lodge secretary Ron Stoate was elected chairman of the South Wales NUM.

CONCLUSION

Penallta is an enduring symbol of a defining chapter in Welsh history. It was one of the few collieries to operate continually from the days of South Wales's pre-eminence as a superpower in global coal production to the virtual extinction of the Welsh coal industry in the 1990s. In the early 20th century, Penallta was the showcase colliery of Powell Duffryn, the largest coal company in Britain. Despite this 'super pit' status though, in other respects Penallta's history strongly mirrored the broader challenges and adversities faced by the South Wales coal industry: dangerous working conditions, industrial relations problems and the ever-present threat of closure. Unlike almost all of the other collieries of South Wales, Penallta colliery was not demolished after it closed. Penallta's survival, in addition to its historical significance in its own right, makes it an important physical reminder of the industry that once defined and dominated South Wales.

Further reading:
Gareth Salway, *Penallta: A Pit and its People* (2008)

18

PARTY AND PROTEST – LIFE IN THE STREET IN MODERN WELSH HISTORY

Paul O'Leary

All events happen *somewhere*, and many of the important events in our modern history have happened in the streets. Usually when we look at towns our attention is attracted by the distinctive buildings they contain. Few of us stop to consider how towns are organized into roads, streets and avenues and the implications of that for the way we behave. Yet the spaces created by streets and the activities that have taken place in them have shaped key aspects of our modern life.

When towns grew and multiplied during the Victorian era, the street became the most important public place in Wales. Streets were places of action and movement. The majority of people now lived in the towns and this is where public life happened for the most of them. The street was where people shopped and walked, where they met to gossip and share news with neighbours and friends. It was where they sometimes listened to speeches and took part in demonstrations. It was also the place where they took part in processions – dressed in their Sunday best – to the accompaniment of musical bands. Walking – whether casually or in a more organized way – put people on display.

Not all streets were the same, of course. As towns grew, residential areas separated out from the commercial streets at the heart of the town. People increasingly lived in one district and worked in another. For much of the 19th century most Welsh towns were 'walking towns'. This meant that it was possible to get from home to work or shops by foot. This changed as the century wore on and trams became a feature of town life, altering the nature of street life and making them more congested with vehicles. By contrast, in the new terraces that accommodated the working-class populations of these growing towns, women often stretched their washing lines between houses. This practice created vistas of fluttering laundry where today there would be cars.

CLEANING THE STREETS

At the beginning of the 19th century Swansea was the largest town in Wales. Its main streets reflected its prosperity as a commercial centre and a resort for tourists. In 1833 it was described by a guide book as being 'modern and well-built'. Its main avenues were broad and well paved and lighted with gas. At the same time, however, the cleaning of the town was 'very defective' and some of the streets were 'deep in mud'. Even so, Swansea probably had the best-kept streets in Wales at that time.

Other places had very different urban environments. Merthyr Tydfil was the Welsh town that most clearly epitomised the changes brought about by the Industrial Revolution. It was a 'shock town' that fascinated and repelled observers in equal measure.

Pontypridd Miners' Procession, 1910

155

MIDDLE-OF-THE-ROAD MERTHYR

In 1850 a visitor to Merthyr thought there was only one street worthy of the name – the High Street. In his opinion, all the others were nothing better than industrial tramroads. He described the practice of its townspeople walking down the middle of the road because of the human waste that was thrown onto the pavements and the absence of proper arrangements for walking down the sides of the streets. 'Entering the town' he wrote, 'you observe a large throng of people moving lazily along the middle of the street, for the pavements, where such exist, are so narrow, and the trap doors so rickety, that walking on them is neither safe nor convenient.'

Natives of Merthyr could be recognised easily when they went elsewhere because of this habit of walking down the middle of the road rather than on the pavements. The nature of Merthyr's streets influenced its inhabitants' behaviour.

Most Welsh towns lay between the two extremes of Merthyr and Swansea, but all had problems of public health. In many cases, conditions varied widely within towns. In Cardiff in the 1840s there was a big difference between the condition of the main streets and the crowded courts and alleyways that lay behind them. The main streets were clear and airy, while the courts and alleyways that existed behind them were cramped and overpopulated. But both types of street required urgent attention to deal with the problem of flooding that plagued the town at this time. When the flood waters receded, townspeople were greeted with the sight and smell of human waste flowing through the streets.

Striking miners take to the street in Tonypandy, 1910

Unsurprisingly, cleaning the streets and improving public health were major concerns. A series of epidemics – cholera and typhus, especially – were brutal reminders of the cost of neglecting the provision of clean water and the condition of the streets. At Cardiff between August 1851 and July 1859 some £16,300 was spent on improvements to the streets in an attempt to improve sanitation and remove nuisances. Towns from Bangor and Wrexham to Newport and Neath made similar investments.

Population growth changed the scale and geography of towns. In a few places, this growth was planned. This was the case in Tredegar, where the town developed a distinctive character. It was organised around a circle at the heart of the settlement with streets leading off it. But this was the exception. New growth caused major problems for most Welsh towns. Most grew in a more or less haphazard way and it was difficult to plan for sudden growth. For example, between 1870 and 1878 Cardiff witnessed the building of as many as 82 new streets – more than ten a year. These contained 3,622 houses, 93 shops, 14 places of worship, 15 new schools, and 919 other buildings. Even at Swansea a critic wrote in 1883 of 'the utterly disgraceful and neglected condition of the streets of this town'. He complained that the better residential streets were looked after but that elsewhere the streets were poorly maintained and potentially dangerous in the dark. Vigilance was the price of clean and well maintained streets.

DISGUSTED OF CARDIFF

The Victorian obsession with the state of the streets is illustrated by an irate reader's letter to the *Western Mail* in 1869, who complained about the state of Cardiff's streets. Recently the weather had been hot and dusty, and the town hadn't made enough provision for damping the dust on the streets. As a result, the clothes of people walking on the pavements were messed up and goods displayed outside shops were ruined.

At times, then, the streets were a source of annoyance.

CIVILIZING THE STREETS

If streets were to be cleaned, then the behaviour of people who used them had to be controlled. They could be dangerous places that often alarmed and unsettled people. During the mid-19th century the creation of county police forces introduced a new figure on to the streets: the local bobby. Some towns – like Aberystwyth – opposed the new police on the grounds that the need for policing reflected badly on a locality. But they were swimming against the tide. Policing the streets was here to stay.

157

The police had a dual mandate: to solve crime and to control behaviour. It was the second of these that sometimes caused tensions between people and police. Solving the problem of public drunkenness was a major concern of the police in the 19th century. Attempting to turn the streets into regulated and orderly spaces was one of the central objectives of the police. The streets had to be 'civilised'.

CONFLICT IN THE STREETS

One of the most influential interpretations of modern Welsh history emphasises the frequency of social conflict in our past. This has sometimes been seen as revealing the radicalism of the Welsh in their quest for social justice and political rights for all.

Since the French Revolution, governments across Europe had feared the prospects of crowds of people congregating in the streets because such groups embodied freedom of action and democracy. They were also a threat to the status quo and to entrenched social and political interests. Welsh history furnishes a number of examples of these clashes. The armed revolt at Merthyr in 1831 and the Chartist Rising at Newport in 1839 are simply two famous examples of this. They demonstrate how people have used the streets at key moments to assert their freedoms against the power of employers and the state. However, the limitations of these two important political events are shown when we look at the urban context in which they occurred.

Both came to grief when the people challenged military power by occupying the streets. This happened outside the Castle Inn at Merthyr in 1831 and the Westgate Hotel at Newport in 1839, when a number of the protesters were shot dead. The streets funnelled people to a point of conflict which allowed the soldiers to fire into the crowd and defeat the rebels with ease. The streets determined the shape of these events. The same is true of the Rebecca Riots in west Wales in the 1830s and 1840s. In this case, the rioters challenged the use of expensive toll gates on the rural roads of west Wales. While they operated in the countryside they were able to avoid the authorities. But when they rode into the streets of Carmarthen in 1843 and were confronted by the military they were easily dispersed. Once again, the streets channelled people and made them easy targets.

It is easier to celebrate and commemorate the occasions of political protest and industrial action – like the famous riots at Tonypandy in 1910 and Llanelli in 1911 – than it is to remember examples of street conflict that leave a bitter taste in the mouth. The anti-Irish riots that took place at Cardiff in

1848 and Tredegar in 1882 were occasions when violence and aggression were channelled through the streets to attack houses and places of worship associated with an ethnic minority. There were similar attacks on Jewish shopkeepers at Tredegar and the Chinese community of Cardiff in 1911, while the black communities of several towns in South Wales were subjected to violence in 1919. The fact that these actions took place on the streets shaped the events in important ways. This urban context determined how and where people congregated, their possibilities for movement and what targets they chose. For members of these minorities, then, the streets were hostile and dangerous territory on particular occasions.

CELEBRATING IN THE STREETS

Conflict, crises and riots are only part of our history. Few societies can exist in permanent crisis, and Wales is no exception. The use of the streets for celebrations reveals a different picture to that of riots and rebellion, and one that tells us a great deal about the less talked about features of public life. For example, during the 20th century the street party became one of the iconic experiences of life in working-class neighbourhoods. Street parties were

Celebrating the 2011 Grand Slam at the big screen in Cardiff's Civic Centre

The fans flock to Cardiff Bay to salute the 2011 Grand Slam winners

organized to celebrate key moments in public life. Across Wales trestle tables loaded with food were set up to mark events such as Victory in Europe (VE) Day, at the end of the war in Europe in 1945. Royal celebrations also brought the sandwich makers onto the streets, with the Coronation of 1951 and the Investiture of the Prince of Wales in 1969 standing out as being particularly significant. These expressions of effusive loyalty to the throne raise serious questions about the interpretation that sees Wales as a particularly radical nation.

These community parties were also opportunities to decorate the streets with flags and bunting, a practice with a much longer historical tradition. In the 19th century townspeople erected ceremonial arches in the main streets to mark particular occasions. This was the case when the Third Marquis of Bute (owner of Cardiff Castle) came of age in September 1868 and there were organized festivities and processions in Cardiff to celebrate the event. The same thing happened when royalty visited Swansea in the 1880s. On other occasions flags, banners and greenery were used to decorate buildings on either side of the street. This practice suggests that the participants in these events saw the streets as their own space, to be adorned for festive events. It is a practice that continues to the present day in the form of Christmas decorations.

Decorating the streets in this manner frequently took place in preparation for peaceful processions by a wide variety of voluntary organisations. These included benefit societies, temperance organisations, Sunday schools and the Rifle Volunteers (the forerunner of the Territorial Army). When we add the major street processions that took place to celebrate the opening of docks and other public works, as well as to mark civic occasions, it is clear that there was a lively culture of street processions. Large funeral processions were another feature of street life. The crowds of observers who lined the pavements were also part of these celebrations. The point was made by a commentator at Swansea who objected to the use of barricades to keep back the crowds. He insisted that barricades 'spring out of the ground when the people despair', while another writer argued that they were 'an interference with the liberty of the subject'.

Peaceful street processions represented big ideals and embodied important aspirations, both for participants and for observers. An illustration of this is the centenary celebrations of the Sunday school movement that took place across the country in June and July in 1880. The processions organised for these celebrations probably brought a higher proportion of the people onto the streets than for any other occasion in Welsh history. And yet until recently it appeared in no history book. If we put these actions in the streets at the centre of our story of modern Wales we get a very different interpretation of our past from the one we're familiar with. It's an interpretation that emphasises the building of civic society rather than one which is shaped by protest and conflict. And the street is at its heart.

CARS AND THE STREETS

Since the 1960s the streets have been transformed by the motor car. It has changed the way citizens use the streets because we no longer walk the streets in the way earlier generations once did. Our oil economy has made public spaces less friendly to pedestrians. There are fewer opportunities to use the streets for processions and celebrations, fewer occasions when people organise themselves in mass activities. This can be seen as an erosion of fundamental freedoms. On the positive side, however, there have been fewer riots and mass violence in our recent history than was once the case. The surveillance society, in tandem with the car, has brought some benefits, controversial though they undoubtedly are.

Nevertheless, one element of continuity is the anxiety we still see about behaviour on the streets. Fears about weekend binge-drinking and brawling in our town centres echo the concerns of Victorians who were alarmed at public drunkenness. But the car has changed our relationship with public spaces in decisive ways. In some towns the creation of pedestrian areas is a recognition that separate spaces have to be set aside for activities that previously jostled with traffic for public attention. The age of the street is not over, but the activities that go on there have changed.

Further Reading

Paul O'Leary, *Claiming the Streets: Processions and Urban Culture in South Wales, c.1830–1880* (2012)

The shoppers of Queen Street, Cardiff

19

WHERE BEVAN GOT HIS PLAN – TREDEGAR

Steven Thompson

Many towns in Wales will lay claim to historical significance or contemporary importance. Merthyr Tydfil, for example, points to its role as the crucible of the British industrial revolution and its importance in the creation of a working-class political identity in Wales. Cardiff boasts of its superior size, its capital status and the important functions of state that are exercised there. In mid-Wales, Aberystwyth declares itself the cultural capital of Wales with its university, National Library and various other bodies and activities. Further north, Caernarfon has its long tradition of Welsh-language publishing and takes pride in its status as the largest Welsh-speaking town in the country.

Few towns, however, can claim quite the same influence as Tredegar. For it was in this particular town that an idea was developed and took root that affected the lives of countless millions of people across Britain and indeed many other countries in different parts of the world. It was an idea that determined the quality of life of generations of British people, from the cradle to the grave, and is one that is fought over in bitter and continuing political and ideological battles to this day.

The idea, of course, was the provision of health services, free at the point of use, in times of need rather than according to the ability to pay, to all citizens as a right and not a privilege, and according to the highest standards of medical science. Many individuals have insisted that Tredegar can lay claim to be the birthplace of the National Health Service because of the efforts to provide health-care to the town's people during the late 19th and early 20th centuries and the influence of these efforts on Aneurin Bevan who, as Minister of Health, was the architect of the new service launched in 1948.

EARLY MEDICAL SCHEMES

Tredegar's influence on the national service came in the form of the Tredegar Workmen's Medical Aid Society. In an age before national health provision, it was common for groups of workers to band together to procure medical care for themselves and their families, and the organisation that made such provision in Tredegar, similar to those in other communities in the Monmouthshire valleys, was one of the most sophisticated and comprehensive in Britain. The people of the town succeeded in creating a medical service for themselves, despite considerable difficulties and challenges, that was the equal of any scheme in Britain at the time.

These working-class medical organisations had their roots in the early period of industrialisation in the late 18th and early 19th centuries, when employers in the burgeoning iron industry appointed surgeons to care for workers and their families, and deducted sums of money from their wages with which to pay the surgeons' salaries. As these iron communities, in places such as Ebbw Vale, Rhymney, Blaenavon and Tredegar, switched to steel and coal production in the second half of the 19th century so struggles were waged by the workmen to wrest control of these medical schemes from their employers.

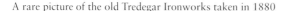

A rare picture of the old Tredegar Ironworks taken in 1880

Workers resented the control exercised by their employers over the appointment and dismissal of doctors, and often made the point that while they paid the piper, they never got to call the tune. They compared their situation to slaves or cattle, sold wholesale to surgeons who had little interest in the standard of care they provided since they could not be dismissed by the patients who paid their salaries. Workers also feared, and with good reason, that in some cases their employers made a profit on the deductions from their wages each week, though there is evidence to suggest that some employers, more paternalistically inclined, subsidised the schemes when deductions were insufficient to pay the surgeons.

Where workers were able to gain control, they looked to institute set salaries for their surgeons and then utilised the resultant surplus to develop further the services available to their members. In this way, the idea of profit was supplanted and any excess in the money raised did not make its way in to the pockets of surgeons or industrialists but was used to develop other forms of provision that would improve the lives of members.

THE TREDEGAR WORKMEN'S MEDICAL AID SOCIETY

In Tredegar's case, the miners and steelworkers who made up the membership of the scheme took control in in the late 19th century. Initially confined to workers employed by the Tredegar Iron and Coal Company, the scheme was extended in future years so as to include the wives and children of members, the elderly in the community, and other workers in the town such as railwaymen, teachers, shopkeepers and others. Miners and steelworkers paid a weekly subscription of two pence in each pound of their wages, while 'town subscribers' were required to pay 18 shillings a year.

The Society even attempted to protect the unemployed during the interwar economic depression. By that time, there were over 2,000 unemployed individuals in Tredegar and the number of subscribers was cut in half. And yet the scheme continued to offer its services to these unemployed individuals, despite the financial difficulties this caused. By the mid-1940s, it was estimated that the Society provided medical care for 22,800 of the town's 24,000 inhabitants thus making it a comprehensive scheme that covered, in effect, the entire population. As one member commented, 'We don't have one medical service for the rich and another for the poor here. What we have is an all-round service for all comers'.

The coverage of the scheme was matched by the breadth of the services it offered to its members. All such schemes in South Wales offered the services of a doctor to their members but some of the more sophisticated versions, particularly in Monmouthshire, were able to channel money into the development of far more comprehensive medical services for their members.

By the 1920s, the Society offered its members the services of five doctors, one surgeon, two pharmacists, a physiotherapist, a dentist, and a district nurse. For an additional 4d. a week, members were covered for hospital treatment, either at the Tredegar Cottage Hospital that had been established with the assistance of the Society and opened in 1904 or at larger hospitals at Newport, Cardiff, Bristol, Bath, Hereford and London, where more specialised medical skill was available. A car was provided to the railway station where a first-class ticket was made available to reach the hospital.

A little later, sun-ray treatment, ultra-violet treatment and expert massage were made available, and it was possible to be sent to a spa or a convalescent home, at no cost, if that particular type of care was needed. Members' wives could enter the county maternity home to which the Society paid a subscription, while glasses could be obtained for 2s. 6d. and false teeth, bath-chairs, bed-sits, air cushions and dietary supplements were supplied at cost price. Artificial limbs, injections, patent foods, drugs, X-rays, and even wigs were all free to members. As a member of the scheme commented in 1946 'It's the only scheme in the country that gives you all the National Health Service sets out, and more'.

THE ROLE OF ANEURIN BEVAN

One of Bevan's biographers described the valleys of South Wales during the early decades of the 20th century as 'test-tubes of Socialism' where it was possible to experiment with different forms of social provision that was intended to better people's lives. And many writers and observers in the early 20th century did indeed look to South Wales for inspiration and ideas

---

EXPERIMENTS EAST AND WEST

Political and Economic Planning, an influential think-tank that looked into the matter of health services in Britain in the 1930s, described the Llanelli and District Medical Service, an organisation very similar to the Tredegar scheme, as 'a comprehensive medical service which should be the measure of any national system of medical services'. Likewise, after the NHS bill was presented to Parliament in 1946, *Picture Post*, an illustrated weekly magazine with a strongly progressive bent, ran a feature on the Tredegar scheme under the title 'Where Bevan got his National Health Plan' and described it as 'one of the most remarkable experiments in health service that this country has seen'.

Tredegar's old Whitworth colliery

in their attempts to solve the problems that afflicted British society, especially during the 1930s when a consensus began to emerge that a significant amount of reform was needed to tackle the considerable problems that were accumulating in too many areas of British life.

Bevan was born and raised in Tredegar, worked as a miner with the Tredegar Iron and Coal Company, and, significantly, served on the Tredegar Hospital Management Committee that was so closely associated with the Medical Aid Society. He was able to observe at first-hand the ways in which working people procured medical care for themselves through this particular organisation. It was not long before he was returned to Parliament as MP for Ebbw Vale, a constituency that included Tredegar and quickly made a name for himself in the Commons as a vocal and effective member of the Labour opposition to the National governments of the 1930s and Churchill's wartime administrations. To the surprise of a great many people, Bevan was appointed Minister of Health in Attlee's government after a landslide election victory in 1945.

It is here, of course, where Tredegar's influence on the National Health Service is to be found. The Beveridge Report of 1942 had called for a national health service but had not suggested what form it should take, while the wartime coalition had also set out some ideas on a national service that might be established in the post-war period but these too were vague and undeveloped. Bevan, it was clear, had very definite ideas about the health service he wished to create and quickly set about the enormously difficult task of negotiating the considerable obstacles placed in his way. He was undoubtedly influenced and guided by his experiences in South Wales and was very much a product of the specific industrial, political and ideological influences that acted upon him in his early life. His intimate knowledge of the Tredegar Workmen's Medical Aid Society led him to emulate its spirit even if he rejected certain aspects of its essential form.

This was evident in a meeting in January 1946 when representatives of the medical aid societies in South Wales met with Bevan and pressed the case that they be allowed to continue to function under the new national scheme. In response, Bevan recognised the important role played by such organisations as the Tredegar Workmen's Medical Aid Society and told them that 'I know the valuable services rendered by Associations. I have been closely associated with them for many years, even from boyhood'.

PEOPLE NOT INSTITUTIONS

When asked if societies such as that at Tredegar were now to be thrown on the scrapheap, Bevan answered 'I very much appreciate the splendid work you have done and are still doing. I am not emotional about Institutions but I am about people'. In a fitting tribute to the significant influence of such organisations, Bevan concluded 'You have shown us the way and by your very efficiency you have brought about your own cessation'.

There were, therefore, various ways in which the new national service differed from that offered in Tredegar but also clear similarities that can be easily discerned. Two of the most obvious similarities, and ones enshrined in the new national service, were universality and collectivist provision. In Tredegar, all but a small number of people were registered with the Society and gained eligibility for care and assistance. A crucial aspect of this universality, and one which marked South Wales schemes out from their counterparts in other parts of Britain, was the poundage system whereby workers paid 2d. or 3d. in each pound of their weekly wages. This meant that better-paid workers contributed more each week than less well-paid members and, as a member of a similar scheme in South Wales commented just before the First World War, 'Now one helps the other, and hundreds and hundreds there are who, if they did not club together in this kind of way, would never be able to get any doctor at all.'

Bevan took these principles of universality and collective provision, and applied them to Britain as a whole. Eligibility was not gained as a result of weekly subscriptions or payments but was instead gained as a right of citizenship, arguably a more generous and inclusive basis for membership than that in Tredegar. Furthermore, the national service was to be funded through general taxation, thereby making collectivist provision in which all contributed according to their means and benefited according to their needs, not according to their ability to pay. As Bevan commented, 'The essence of a satisfactory health service is that the rich and the poor are treated alike, that poverty is not a disability, and wealth is not advantaged'.

The significant differences were, of course, the rejection of local provision and, in place, the harnessing of the powers of the state, through general taxation and central direction, to provide a national service. Bevan was appreciative of all that voluntary organisations and local authorities had achieved in their efforts to provide medical and welfare care but believed that only the state could raise the necessary funds, co-ordinate services across the country, and ensure a measure of fairness and equality for all. Schemes such as that found at Tredegar were of a very high standard and were not replicated elsewhere with the result that the state needed to intervene to raise the standard of health-care for all citizens to this level.

Modern Tredegar

IN PLACE OF FEAR

A number of years after the formation of the NHS, Bevan published a book in which he set out various ideas on the health service he created. The book was entitled *In Place of Fear* and the very title sums up one of the fundamental aims of the Tredegar scheme, the National Health Service and indeed the welfare states created in so many countries in the post-war period. In place of the fear aroused by sickness, injury, high medical bills and poverty, the Tredegar Workmen's Medical Aid Society and the National Health Service both attempted to provide health, well-being and security, and thereby made a profound difference to people's everyday lives. Bevan wrote that the collective principle he attempted to enshrine in the national service 'insists that no society can legitimately call itself civilised if a sick person is denied medical aid because of lack of means'.

At a time when the NHS is under greater threat than ever before, a time when the fundamental principles that have underpinned the service for the entirety of its history are attacked and threatened more than in any period since the service's foundation, there is a need to look again, perhaps, at the situation in Britain before 1948 and the choices and decisions made in the mid-1940s. Tredegar, through its most famous son, and the example of medical provision it provided for him, inspired one of the world's greatest achievements in social welfare provision and a medical scheme that has proven enormously popular to the British people ever since its inception. Wales, and indeed Britain as a whole, owes the town of Tredegar a great deal.

Further reading

Gareth Jones, *The Aneurin Bevan Inheritance: The story of the Nevill Hall and District NHS Trust* (Abertillery, 1998)

20

PANDEMONIUM – MAMETZ WOOD

Robin Barlow

The name of Mametz Wood, perhaps like that of Aberfan or Senghennydd, is embedded deep in the Welsh psyche, immediately conjuring up images of bravery, chaos, self-sacrifice and needless loss of life. Hundreds of Welshmen died at Mametz, most of them volunteers, and thousands more were casualties.

Yet to visit Mametz Wood today, initially it is hard to imagine the violent loss of life that took place in early July 1916 when the Somme offensive was at its height and the 38th (Welsh) Division was tested for the first time in battle. One sees now the neatly ploughed fields, the sleepy villages and the well-tended cottages and gardens. Perhaps the most potent reminder of the Great War is the number of military cemeteries appearing around every corner, with row upon row of uniform headstones stretching into the distance.

Following a footpath into the Wood, the atmosphere changes: there is a chill about the place and little light penetrates the tree canopy, even on the sunniest of days. Shell craters, shallow trenches and other earthworks are still clearly evident, with remnants of rusting barbed wire in amongst the thick undergrowth.

It occupies an area of approximately 220 acres and measures about one mile from north to south and three-quarters of a mile from east to west at its widest point. However the Wood was attacked, it would have involved troops moving down the slope of a valley, then being faced with an uphill advance in open country to reach the enemy.

One of the most striking sights is the Welsh Division memorial – a vivid red dragon, tearing at barbed wire, atop a three-metre granite plinth – which faces across the open fields to Mametz Wood, passively guarding the memory of the hundreds of Welshmen who died here. The memorial was crafted by

Mametz Wood and the Memorial

Welsh sculptor and blacksmith, David Petersen and was unveiled on 11 July 1987. The regimental badges of the South Wales Borderers, the Royal Welsh Fusiliers and the Welsh Regiment are sculpted into the plinth.

THE POETRY OF WAR

Siegfried Sassoon, an officer in the 2nd Battalion Royal Welsh Fusiliers, described moving across the open hillside with Mametz Wood 'looming on the opposite slope... a dense wood of old trees and undergrowth... a menacing wall of gloom'. Harry Fellows, in his poem on Mametz Wood, describes 'A panoply of magnificent trees / Stretching upwards to the skies'.

THE BATTLE OF THE SOMME

The 38th (Welsh) Division, with its distinctive *brethyn llwyd* uniform, had first assembled in North Wales before embarking for France in December 1915. After a quiet introduction to trench warfare in the area around Givenchy, the Division moved to St Pol in preparation for the forthcoming major offensive on the Somme in early July 1916.

Following seven days of heavy bombardment of the German lines, when a million-and-a-half shells were fired, the objective was to capture the German front along an 11-mile stretch from Maricourt to Serre, then continue eastwards and take the German second line from Pozieres to Grandcourt and beyond.

172

This would allow the cavalry to push through in to open country behind the German lines. The capture of Mametz Wood was of great strategic importance as it was seen as the key to a successful attack on the German second line in the area.

The first day of the Battle of the Somme, 1 July 1916, has become symbolic of the apparent futility of the First World War and the blatant devaluation of human life. In a single day, almost 20,000 British soldiers were killed and a further 40,000 were casualties. The artillery bombardment had proved totally ineffective against the deeply embedded German trenches. The gains, such as they were, seemed a paltry reward for the loss of life.

On 5 July, the Welsh Division took over a section of the front line immediately south of Mametz Wood, with orders to prepare for its capture. The odds were certainly not in their favour. The vast majority of the soldiers in the division were amateurs who had volunteered in the heady, patriotic days of September 1914, expecting the war to be over by Christmas. During their training they had suffered from a dire lack of equipment, most notably rifles. Most men had never fired a round on a range, never mind at the enemy, before they embarked for France. For drill practice they had been forced to use broomsticks as a substitute for rifles.

Confronting the 38th Division was the elite Lehr regiment of Prussian Guards – highly trained professional soldiers, equipped with mortars and machine guns. Furthermore they were deeply entrenched on easily defended ground. With typical understatement, the official history commented, 'The task that lay before the Division was one of some magnitude'.

The attack on Mametz Wood began at 08.30 on 7 July. The advance floundered in chaos 200–300 yards short of the Wood, and a further attack at 11.00 met with the same fate.

A third attack was then ordered and an artillery bombardment arranged for 16.30. The rain had continued to fall, the ground was sodden, telephone wires had been cut and progress was extremely difficult.

The decision was made by the commanding officer of the 115th Brigade not to carry out the planned attack. Under the cover of darkness, the bedraggled troops returned to their positions. Llewelyn Wyn Griffith commented bitterly, 'It was nearly midnight when we heard that the last of our men had withdrawn from that ridge and valley, leaving the ground empty, save for the bodies of those who had to fall to prove to our command that machine guns can defend a bare slope'.

At the end of 7 July, the Welsh Division was back in exactly the same position as it had been at dawn that morning, the only difference being that

177 men and three officers had lost their lives. The two battalions which had led the attacks bore the brunt of the casualties: the 11th Battalion, South Wales Borderers lost thirty men, whilst the 16th Battalion (Cardiff City), Welsh Regiment lost 129 men, with 61 of those being Cardiffians.

British Prime Minister David Lloyd George with King George V (right).

174

DEATH NOT TO BE CHEATED

One who died was Cpl Frederick Hugh Roberts, a Senghennydd miner, originally from Bethedsa, who had enlisted in the 16th Battalion, Welsh Regiment early in the war. He had cheated death already once, when a successful bet on a horse had led to a heavy night's drinking and a resultant hangover. This had kept him away from the pit on 17 October 1913 when the worst mining disaster in British history killed 439 of his workmates. Roberts died on 10 July of his wounds and is buried in Heilly Station Cemetery, Mericourt-l'Abbe. His name also appears on the Senghennydd war memorial with 62 other men from the town.

Two of the officers who died were brothers Arthur and Leonard Tregaskis. Having emigrated to Canada, they returned to fight in the war, joined up together, were awarded temporary commissions in the Welsh Regiment on the same day, and died together on 7 July. They are buried side by side in Flatiron Copse Cemetery, Mametz.

The first real test for the volunteer soldiers of the Welsh Division had ended in ignominy and recrimination. Field Marshal Douglas Haig laid the blame for the failed attack squarely at the door of the Welsh Division for not advancing 'with determination to the attack'. Major-Gen. Philipps, the Commanding Officer of the Welsh Division, was held responsible for the failures of 7–9 July and given his marching orders. He was replaced by Major-Gen. Watts who immediately received orders for another attack on Mametz Wood, to begin at 04.15 on 10 July.

There was clearly a feeling amongst many in the Welsh Division that they were on trial after the failures of 7/8 July. Lieutenant-Colonel Hayes, commanding officer of the Swansea Pals, addressed the officers of the Battalion: 'we are going to take that wood, but we shall lose our battalion'.

Yet again the attack was poorly co-ordinated and chaotically executed. Capt Glynn Jones, 14th Battalion, Royal Welsh Fusiliers, at the rear of the attack was able to describe the scene ahead:

> Presently the silent waves of men started moving forward, and I, with my third wave joined in. Machine guns and rifles began to rattle, and there was a general state of pandemonium, little of which I can remember except that I myself was moving down the slope at a rapid rate, with bullet-holes in my pocket and yelling a certain amount.

As the 14th Battalion reached the Wood, Capt Glynn Jones was confronted by about forty German soldiers coming out with their hands up. He thought it was a trick and warily approached them. However, the men were genuinely surrendering, were taken prisoner and sent back to headquarters. During the offensive, the Welsh Division captured 352 prisoners of war, including four officers.

By mid-morning on 10 July, the Welsh Division had gained a solid foothold within the Wood. Throughout the day, the thick undergrowth, poor visibility, well-established machine-gun posts and effective sniper fire had made every yard gained a gargantuan effort. The ferocity of the fighting was described by Emlyn Davies, 17th Battalion, Royal Welsh Fusiliers who had entered Mametz Wood during the afternoon:

> Gory scenes met our gaze. Mangled corpses in khaki and in field-grey; dismembered bodies, severed heads and limbs; lumps of torn flesh halfway up the tree trunks; a Welsh Fusilier reclining on a mound, a red trickle oozing from his bayoneted throat; a South Wales Borderer and a German locked in their deadliest embraces – they had simultaneously bayoneted each other. A German gunner with jaws blown off lay against his machine gun, hand still on its trigger.

As nightfall approached, the bedraggled troops found cover where they could, exhausted after fifteen hours of continuous fighting. At daybreak on 11 July, the Welsh Division was in a state of disarray, scattered throughout the Wood, with many battalions severely depleted.

Llewelyn Wyn Griffith described the scene confronting him in Mametz Wood:

> Equipment, ammunition, rolls of barbed wire, tins of food, gas-helmets and rifles were lying about everywhere. There were more corpses than men, but there were worse sights than corpses. Limbs and mutilated trunks, here and there a detached head, forming splashes of red against the green leaves, and, as in advertisement of the horror of our way of life and death, and of our crucifixion of youth, one tree held in its branches a leg, with its torn flesh hanging down over a spray of leaf.

Two sets of brothers had been killed: Henry and Charles Morgan had both worked at the Blaenavon Steel & Iron Company, joined the 16th Battalion, Welsh Regiment in late 1914 and died together in battle on 7 July. Thomas and Henry Hardwidge, both married men from Ferndale working in the local colliery, enlisted together in the 15th Battalion, Welsh Regiment. On 11 July, Tom Hardwidge was fatally wounded and as his brother went to his aid, he was shot and killed by a German sniper. The brothers lie buried side by side in Flatiron Copse Cemetery.

During the afternoon of 11 July, the decision had been taken at Divisional Headquarters to withdraw the Welsh Division from the battle area. The 38th Division was relieved by the 21st Division, which cleared the remainder of Mametz Wood by midday on 12 July, encountering little resistance. The Welsh Division did not have the satisfaction of seeing the job through and witnessing the total capture of Mametz Wood.

The human toll at the battle of Mametz was a high one. Between 7–12 July, 911 NCOs and other ranks from the Welsh Division lost their lives, plus 37 officers. In addition, many hundreds more men would have been posted missing, their bodies never recovered. The 16th (Cardiff City) Battalion, Welsh Regiment suffered the greatest loss with 153 men and five officers killed, 129 of whom (and three officers) died on 7 July. The 14th (Swansea) Battalion, Welsh Regiment had entered its first major engagement of the First World War on 10 July with 676 men; by nightfall, 75 men and one officer had died, with a further 376 casualties. Over half the battalion was lost in

The Red Dragon keeps watch from the top of the Memorial

one day. The attacking strength of the 17th Battalion, Royal Welsh Fusiliers was recorded as '950 bayonets'; on 12 July Emlyn Davies transmitted a message to 115th Brigade headquarters, 'strength 5 Officers, 142 Other Ranks'.

AFTERMATH

Although the name of Mametz Wood has come to symbolize the sacrifice and commitment of Welsh troops in the First World War, their actual contribution – and even their bravery – is wreathed in controversy and debate. Was it a glorious success or a chaotic failure?

In the words of the officers of a neighbouring division, the advance of the Welsh Division on 10 July was 'one of the most magnificent sights of the war', as wave after wave of men were seen 'advancing without hesitation'. Colin Hughes, after a painstakingly thorough analysis of the battle concluded that,

'...the Welsh Division, inexperienced and inadequately trained, pushed the cream of Germany's professional army back about one mile in most difficult conditions, an achievement that should rank with that of any division on the Somme'.

Others, however, accused the Welsh Division of indiscipline, a failure to follow orders and even cowardice. Brig-Gen. L.A.E. Price Davies, Commanding Officer of the 113th Brigade, was scathing in his criticism of his own troops, describing 'a disgraceful panic during which many left the wood whilst others seemed quite incapable of understanding, or unwilling to carry out the simplest order. A few stout-hearted Germans would have stampeded the whole of the troops in the wood'.

Siegfried Sassoon referred to the 'massacre and confusion', which was 'only a prelude to that pandemonium which converted the green thickets of Mametz Wood to a desolation of skeleton trees and blackened bodies'. Tellingly, he concluded that the battle was 'a disastrous muddle with troops stampeding under machine-gun fire'

The final irony was that within weeks, German troops recaptured Mametz Wood and held it for the remainder of the war. Seemingly, like so many events of the Great War, the bravery of the members of the 38th (Welsh) Division during the battle of the Somme was an exercise in futility. However, this is to ignore the heroism and suffering of thousands of Welshmen, which eventually helped to pave the way for final victory in 1918; their efforts and sacrifice were not in vain.

Further reading:

Colin Hughes, *Mametz, Lloyd George's 'Welsh Army' at the Battle of the Somme*, (1990)

21

HOLY ISLE AND 'KINGDOM OF THE CHIP': BARRY ISLAND

Andy Croll

Barry Island takes up little space on a map. It is a small place. Indeed, in 1997, *The New York Times* described it as a 'stubby peninsula'. This was hardly the most flattering of characterizations, but, weighing-in at a mere 170 acres and with a circumference only a mile-and-a-half in length, it was probably accurate enough. Yet the island's significance cannot be measured by cartographers. Barry Island's claim to be a truly iconic location rests on the fact that it is a place in the collective imagination of generations from South Wales and far beyond.

The fact that readers of *The New York Times* were even reading about Barry Island tells us something important. On the face of it, we might not expect sophisticated Manhattans to have much interest in a little knuckle of rock set in the chilly waters of the Bristol Channel. But, in truth, it should be no surprise that New Yorkers, of all people, would relate to Barry Island. They, after all, had their equivalent in Coney Island – a peninsula a little less 'stubby' than its counterpart at Barry, to be sure, but which fulfilled precisely the same function – as a seaside playground for one of the most important industrial regions the world has ever seen.

In a South Wales shaped by the forces of industrial capitalism and dominated by the workplace, Barry Island stood out as a precious jewel; a standing reminder that there was something more to life than back-breaking labour. It was the paradise of the urban pleasure-seeker and, as such, Barry Island was not only the 'Blackpool of South Wales' (an epithet that was often used to describe it), it really was the Coney Island of South Wales too.

THE 'GAVIN AND STACEY' PHENOMENON

The Island's golden age as a working-class seaside resort extended from the late Victorian period through to 1970s. However, it is important to note that Barry Island's iconic status is not limited to this short moment in history. As we shall see, it was thought of as a special, even sacred, place long before the Victorian era. And, in our own, de-industrialized days, it has enjoyed a remarkable resurgence in its fortunes thanks to a TV sitcom.

Gavin and Stacey has boosted the profile of Whitmore Bay and its environs in a most spectacular fashion. According to the local tourism officer, the show has 'had a huge effect on Barry, helping to put it on the map'. It's certainly had an invigorating effect on visitor numbers. A brand new social type – the 'TV tourist' – has been spotted on the island in ever-increasing numbers.

How many of the 300,000 visitors who descend upon Barry Island annually do so because of the show is uncertain. But a breathtaking number of *Gavin*

An aerial view of Butlin's, Barry Island

and Stacey fans harbour a desire to make the pilgrimage to Barry at some undisclosed point in the future. Surveys reveal that a staggering 3.1 million TV viewers reported an intention to visit the island after watching the sitcom. The car-park attendants must be hoping they don't all turn up on the same day.

By the end of the first decade of the new millennium, some locals have taken to referring to the Island as 'Barrybados'. The neologism catches a truth: 'Barry Island', the brand, has gone global. Ask viewers of *Gavin and Stacey* in Iceland, Belgium, Ireland, the Netherlands, Israel, Sweden, New Zealand, the United States or Portugal to name a place in Wales and, more likely than not, Barry Island will be their response. Never mind just being a Welsh place; for many around the world, Barry Island has come to stand for the whole of Wales.

A MEDIEVAL HOLY ISLAND

In a wonderful example of life imitating art, in 2008, a wedding party from Essex journeyed to Barry declaring that 'they had to visit Barry Island to be able to tell all their friends and fans of the show back in Essex that they had been there'. This act of going to the island to pay homage might seem to be a very recent development, the product of a facile infatuation with TV celebrities. It's not. Its origins lie far back in the early medieval period when the island really was an island – and a holy one, at that.

Barry Island was not joined to the mainland until the very end of the 19th century. Until the navvies arrived, in the 1880s, to excavate the great docks, the island stood aloof in Barry sound. Accessible by foot at low tide only, it was, for centuries, seen as a perfect place to commune with God. Wild, lonely and remote, Barry Island attracted a variety of hermits and holy men.

According to most authorities (almost all of whom are unreliable), one of the earliest of these ascetics went by the name of Peiro. Reportedly a master at organizing others, he set up a small community of monks on the island at some point in the mid-fifth century. The same reports suggest he was less successful at keeping himself in check – 'in private he was not to be admired', one 17th-century Benedictine scribe hinted darkly. We can only guess what vices could be indulged, in private, on fifth-century Barry Island; how a 17th-century Benedictine monk would know about them also remains an unanswered question.

All this religious activity, not to mention the miraculous salmon, marked Barry Island out as a site of especial importance in the Middle Ages. Pilgrims flocked to the island for hundreds of years, worshipping in the little chapel that

SAINT BARUCH, SAINT CADOC AND THE SUPERSIZED SALMON

The island would probably have still been called Ynys Peiro if it had not been for the tragic story of St Baruch – another holy resident of Whitmore Bay. Baruch was a follower St Cadoc. One day, Cadoc and Baruch set sail from Flat Holm to Barry Island. Unfortunately, Baruch made the fatal mistake of forgetting to pack his master's holy manual. On arrival at Barry Island, Cadoc discovered Baruch's error, flew into an unholy rage, and sent the absent-minded young man back to collect the book. En route, the hapless monk's boat was engulfed in a choppy Bristol Channel. Cadoc's precious book and Baruch were both drowned.

A few hours later, Baruch's body was washed up on the sands of Whitmore Bay. Seemingly unfazed by the traumatic events of the day, Cadoc's thoughts turned to food and he ordered his attendants to go fishing. What they found was nothing less than a giant salmon washed up on the beach. In its bowels they discovered Cadoc's lost book, remarkably 'free from all injury by water'.

took Baruch's name, and leaving offerings at various holy wells. Baruch's Isle was significant enough for Giraldus Cambrensis to include it in his description of late 12th-century Wales, although it is unlikely that Gerald actually visited it. We can be certain that many others did though. When archaeologists visited the Island in the late 19th century, they estimated that some several thousand bodies had been interred in the shadow of the chapel over the generations. They had all been carried over to Barry Island after their death.

THE DISCOVERY OF WHITMORE BAY

It is tempting to think of Barry Island as a medieval seaside resort. The image of hundreds of pilgrims frolicking in the waters of Whitmore Bay after a day of pious worship is an appealing one. Sadly, it's also deeply unhistorical. For as historians have shown, there was an entrenched fear of the sea at this time. The deep waters were thought to be filled with fantastical monsters. The sea was also seen as an instrument of a vengeful God – the story of Noah showed that only too clearly. And devotees of the drowned St Baruch needed no reminding of just how dangerous the swirling currents of the Bristol Channel could be.

Strange as it may seem to us, for large swathes of human history, the beach was a place to avoid – a wild and unpredictable space. All this changed of course, but only recently. Not until the 18th century do we see a profound transformation in attitudes. Learned treatises extolled the health-giving properties of seawater. Some experts went as far as recommending it be quaffed by the pint. Others were content merely to prescribe immersion in the sea as a treatment for a bewildering array of medical conditions.

As the well-to-do started to see the seaside in new ways, fashionable resorts popped up around the coast of Britain. But not at Barry. It remained an outpost of sullen remoteness – home to an impressive colony of rabbits, but, now that the pilgrims had stopped coming, barely disturbed by human activity. One visitor, in 1803, wrote that Whitmore Bay 'inspired melancholy'; it was not a place he could recommend to his readers.

In the 19th century, the island passed through the hands of various owners including the eccentric Francis Crawshay. Son of the great Merthyr family of ironmasters, Crawshay had his main residence at Treforest just south of Pontypridd. A love of the sea and of sailing prompted him to purchase the island. Once installed there, he erected a summer home out of the flotsam and jetsam of old shipwrecks on Friars Point.

Crawshay's Island was on the maps of at least some early and mid-Victorian day-trippers. There are scattered references in the newspapers to various groups of visitors: a 'geological excursion' organized by the Cardiff Young Men's Christian Association in the 1850s; a Sunday school picnic at Whitmore Bay in 1871; a works outing for employees of the Cambrian Engine and Tugboats Works in 1873. By this time, bathing was indulged in by some too. But it was not until work on the docks began in 1884 that the little island at Barry really came into its own as a seaside resort.

Welsh summers were so much warmer back then!

'THE BLACKPOOL OF SOUTH WALES'

Late Victorian South Wales was no stranger to rapid urban growth, but what happened at Barry was quite remarkable. In 1881, there were 85 souls living in the Barry district. Within twenty years, this figure had mushroomed to some 27,000. At the eve of the First World War the population was heading towards 40,000. By that time, not only had Barry become the world's greatest coal exporting port, it was also well on the way to establishing itself as the premier working-class seaside resort in South Wales.

The working class of the South Wales coalfield had already cultivated a love of the seaside. A committed few journeyed to Aberystwyth to satiate their demand for saline pleasures. Many more took advantage of the newly instituted bank holidays and flocked, by rail, to Penarth in the 1880s and early 1890s. However, the reception they received at the hands of bourgeois Penarthians was even chillier than the waters that lapped at the town's pebbly beach. They needed little inducement to switch allegiances to Barry Island. In fact, all it took was a railway link.

The Barry Dock Company changed Barry Island for ever. For one thing, it connected the island to the mainland for the first time in tens of thousands of years. Even more profoundly, the linking of Barry to the wider rail network meant that Whitmore Bay was at last within easy reach of hundreds of thousands of day-trippers from the coalfield. As news of the island's delights spread, Barry began drawing workers from the English Midlands too.

Something for all the family!

The chronology of the resort's rise as a seaside resort is easily described. The island passed from private hands to the Barry Council in the early years of the 20th century. The interwar period saw sustained investment in the built form of Whitmore Bay. A stone sea-wall replaced an older wooden structure. The sand dunes were refashioned into ornamental gardens. Shelters and bandstands were thrown up. And the funfair, by now in the hands of the Collins family, added ever more attractions to entice and thrill the day-trippers. After the Second World War, the resort went from strength to strength. Visitor numbers boomed. On the August Bank Holiday of 1950, over 120,000 were crammed onto the sands. There was nothing unusual about that year. In the mid-1960s, a Butlin's holiday camp opened, bringing yet more visitors to the Island.

It is one thing to chart the growth of day-tripper numbers but quite another to explain the magical allure of Barry Island. Some might point to the considerable natural charms of Whitmore Bay. Others might offer a geographical explanation. The island was close to a major centre of population – it was bound to become the beach playground of South Wales at some point. Maybe. But there are prettier spots along the coast and, as the example of the snooty Penarth shows, a beach close to the coalfield was, on its own, no guarantee of tourist success.

To understand why the island came to occupy such a privileged place in the affections of innumerable South Walians, we need to think more imaginatively. Fortunately, Gwyn Thomas, novelist and interpreter of the coalfield experience, has done much of the thinking for us. Thomas, born in the Rhondda in 1913 and long-time resident of Barry, was better placed than most to understand the peculiar appeal of Whitmore Bay. The answer for him lay, at least in part, in the striking contrast between the topography of the valleys and that of the seaside: 'the sea hinted at a possible escape to infinity, hills did not block out the sky, men did not vanish into holes in the ground.' Furthermore, whilst he detected a 'coldness' at Porthcawl, he 'felt more at home in the loose, lusty jacket of Whitmore Bay'.

'THE KINGDOM OF THE CHIP'

Of course, not everyone liked Barry Island. As Gwyn Thomas pointed out, some Barrians themselves were appalled at the tackiness of the 'Kingdom of the Chip'. For them, the cheap cafes, the fairground rides, the saucy postcards and the donkey rides represented a depressing despoliation of Whitmore Bay. Luckily, their more genteel sensibilities were catered for at Barry's Cold Knap and Porthkerry Park.

But Gwyn Thomas was perfectly attuned to the popular taste. He understood instinctively the deep significance of Barry Island for the working-class day-trippers. It was a place of 'colourful recreation' that satisfied the 'very real hungers felt in lives that [had] been pressed squat by an excess of disciplined labour and social dreariness'. He thought that the Island wore the past 'like a robe of rustling laughter'.

And it is because Barry Island delighted, amused, relaxed and excited generations of those remarkable men, women and children who made South Wales one of the most important industrial centres in the world that we should cherish it today as a place as sacred and as special as ever it was in the days of the medieval hermits.

If you want to visit a genuinely iconic Welsh place, then look no further than Barry Island: the 'stubby peninsula' that is the resting place of holy St Baruch, the home of Stacey, Nessa and Uncle Bryn, and, most importantly of all, the Coney Island of South Wales.

Further Reading:

John K Walton, *The British Seaside: Holidays and Resorts in the Twentieth Century* (2000)

22

THE WAY AHEAD – THE M4

Martin Johnes

Roads do not often get much attention from historians but they are central to the lives of individuals and the M4 has been central to the life of post-war Wales. In its earliest days, it was appreciated as a modern marvel and its construction is an engineering feat as important as any canal or railway.

A South Wales without the M4 is now unimaginable. It enables the economy of South Wales to function. It has become engrained in the physical and mental landscape. The time before it, a time of tailbacks and long journeys, a time not actually that long ago, has been forgotten.

THE HISTORIC ROAD NETWORK

Before the motorway, the main route into England from South Wales was the A48. It ran from Gloucester to Carmarthen and passed through the centres of Cardiff, Newport and Swansea. There were sharp turns, steep hills and varying road widths to slow down traffic. On the stretch between Gloucester and Chepstow there were 10 steep hills, 3 narrow bridges, 4 low bridges, 2 sharp bends, 5 danger spots and 1 badly designed junction.

Upgrading this road system was discussed in the 1930s as a way of integrating depressed South Wales into more prosperous economies of the Midlands and southern England. Government first approved the concept of a motorway system in 1942 and a route from London to Swansea, including a bridge across the Severn, was part of its plans. However, financial constraints held back any significant progress until the 1950s.

As that decade progressed, the need for a new road network increased. Coal and steel had always been reliant on the railways but economic policy now centred on developing Welsh manufacturing. This sector depended on roads to bring parts in and move finished products out.

More lorries on the roads added to the strain on a road network that was also struggling to cope with the rising number of private cars that 1950s affluence brought. By 1960 average speeds through Cardiff were below 20 mph. In Newport they could fall as low as 7 mph at peak hours. This was the road network upon which the South Wales economy depended.

BUILDING THE MOTORWAY

In 1953 Wales's first motorway was announced: the Port Talbot bypass. It was a logical place to start. The A48 snaked through the town on a route that dated back to the days of horse-and-carts. It had to cross a railway which meant it was shut for three hours a day, causing tailbacks of several miles. The result was that for a 5½ mile stretch on the A48 the average car speed was 18 mph. Traffic was worsening too after the town's new steelworks opened in 1951.

Building a major new road was not quick and it was not until July 1966 that the 4.5 mile A48(M) opened. It cut the journey time between Swansea and Cardiff by twenty minutes. For those who were not having to contemplate living beside the motorway, it was difficult not to be impressed by how it ran over the town on 45-foot-high gleaming white concrete pillars.

The *Western Mail* produced a six-page supplement to mark its opening, called it a '£5m miracle' and claimed that it would become 'one of the sights of Wales'. The Town Clerk proclaimed 'if you stand still you die, and Port Talbot intends to live.'

The road was thus a symbol of progress, a modern marvel that saved time and demonstrated the practical benefits to ordinary people of the age's technological developments. It also hastened demands for further motorways.

Other sections were already in construction and the Severn Bridge and Newport bypass soon opened in 1966 and 1967 respectively. The remaining parts of the M4 were gradually completed over the next quarter century. In 1977, 30 miles were completed and the *Western Mail* concluded it had been 'the most momentous year for road building in South Wales since the Romans left'. But it was not until 1994 and the filling in of the Baglan to Lôn Las 'missing link' that the 80-mile stretch of the M4 in South Wales was actually finished.

Yet, by the 21st century, the short-sightedness of savings made by building some sections of the M4 with two rather than three lanes was apparent and congestion was again a significant problem.

Plans for a relief motorway across the Gwent Levels were abandoned because of cost and the environmental impact but other new upgrades had to be implemented around Cardiff to bring the motorway up to three lanes in one of its busiest sections. Like so many historic sites, motorways do not remain unchanged.

THE SEVERN BRIDGES

By the 1980s, motorway engineers sometimes seemed rather annoyed that their achievements were not widely heralded. The initial pleasure and amazement with motorways quickly faded, as the roads became engrained into daily life and their time savings were forgotten and eroded by ever rising traffic levels.

This was clearest with the original Severn Bridge (actually two bridges, one across the Severn and one across the Wye). It was the seventh largest bridge in the world, cut the road distance between London and Cardiff by 18 miles and between Bristol and Cardiff by 55 miles. It was a masterpiece of engineering.

The St Julian Viaduct at Newport, 1965

Its opening generated huge crowds and genuine excitement. On its first Sunday there was chaos and five-mile tailbacks. The police had to ask motorists to avoid the bridge unless they had to cross. Collisions became commonplace, with drivers looking around at the bridge rather than at the road ahead of them. In August 1967, a survey estimated that 12% of traffic across the Severn was people specifically setting out to see the bridge. It had the aura of something glamorous and American about it and it quickly became a powerful symbol of the modernization of Wales and its economy. In 1998, the bridge was made a grade 1 listed building.

But not everyone was enamoured with this new marvel. There were some in the 1960s who feared that it would further the cultural integration of Wales into England. The Free Wales Army even threatened to blow it up.

More rational people also quickly became disillusioned. There were regular delays caused by high winds and maintenance work. Its success also meant far more traffic than had ever been anticipated. The Severn Bridge had been intended to carry 5 to 10 million crossings a year, but by 1996 there were 18 million.

At peak times there could be a six-mile queue of vehicles waiting to pay their tolls, which themselves always seemed to be going up. Had tolls increased at the rate of inflation between 1966 and 2009 it would only have cost around £1.75 to cross. The actual toll was £5.40.

IT TOLLS FOR THEE

To relieve the traffic but not the toll problem, a second Severn bridge was opened in 1996. Its cost, including the approach roads, was £428.3m. Some of this was borne by private investment in return for the right to charge tolls and the main route in and out of Wales was privatized. However, the tolls were only paid when entering Wales, something which became the subject of both humour and anger.

THE POLITICS OF MOTORWAYS

Motorways were always political. The most significant advances came after the creation of the Welsh Office in 1964 when there was a government department that put Wales first. But it still had to argue with London to get the money to do anything about it. That was easier said than done and the time it took to build the M4 illustrates how either political or administrative devolution can only really be effective if it is properly resourced.

The politics of road building had become clear in the 1950s when the Forth Bridge was given priority over the Severn Bridge because of the perceived political needs of the Conservative government. In compensation to Wales, the M50 was commissioned. That road was important in opening up the Midlands to Wales but the need for it was limited and it remains one of the quietest motorways in the UK.

It was at a far more local level that roads were most obviously political. In Port Talbot the M4 brutally dissected the town and required the demolition of three chapels and more than 200 houses. With ten years between the planning inquiry and the actual beginning of construction, there was a good deal of confusion over what was happening, especially as plans had to be changed to meet developing design requirements. Some tenants only found out that their homes were scheduled for demolition through rumours or from the newspaper.

Letters were written to the Ministry of Transport. Some suggested alternative routes, while others worried about losing their garage or shed or just wanted to know when they'd have to move. The Ministry did deal sensitively with the objections, even visiting people to explain the situation and trying to find one individual surplus land where a new garage could be built. But that did not stop the compulsory purchases and the requirement for people to leave their homes, often at little notice.

The Brynglas Tunnels under construction in 1966

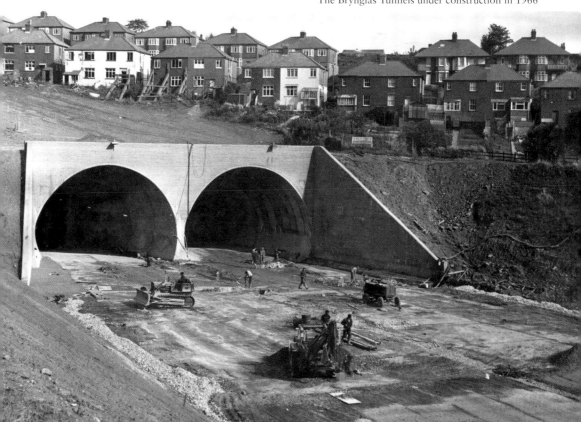

For those not losing their homes but living on the doorstep of the new road things could be worse. Some found their view change from a terrace of neighbours to a huge concrete wall on top of which ran a noisy, dirty motorway. Quite apart from the intrusion and disruption of the years of construction, their community and lives were changed irrevocably. Unlike those whose homes were affected by the stages of the M4 built after the 1973 Land Compensation Act, they got not a single penny in compensation.

Yet people accepted the whole situation with remarkable fortitude and calmness. There was no scandal or organized campaign of opposition. One pensioner, who was losing his home of 40 years, noted that it was 'tragic' but the road was needed. Modernization was the dominant rhetoric of the 1950s and 1960s and the working classes were not going to speak up en masse against projects that would create jobs and develop the economy. Indeed, the population of South Wales was used to suffering environmental harm in the name of progress.

Nor did many outsiders seem to care much. In Groes near Port Talbot, the 1970s extension of the M4 saw all 21 houses in the village demolished, although its historic round chapel was moved to another site. In stark contrast to the campaign against the flooding of the Welsh-speaking village Cwm Celyn in the late 1950s, this small working-class community got little more than sympathy from outsiders. A *Western Mail* editorial concluded 'The disturbance of existing communities is often a sad but unavoidable consequence of motorway building.'

A SYMBOL OF THE NATION(S)

Although economists argued over the precise benefits, the M4 came to be seen as an economic lifeline that joined South Wales to the rest of Britain. It boosted economic development in those towns close to it. In Cardiff, the local authorities invested significant resources in building link roads to ensure the motorway's benefits would not bypass the city.

Further west, the M4's economic impact was less stark because of the greater distance from English markets. However, in the industrial valleys, the M4 fed some feeling of marginalization because of the way economic development in the south clustered along the motorway corridor.

The M4 thus raised questions about road links within Wales. The southern section of the A470 grew in importance and congestion because not only did it link the Valleys to Cardiff but to the M4 and thus the wider world too. In both North and South Wales, the main routes run east-west, and north-south links within Wales remain extremely poor. The environmental arguments against a major new highway to unite north and south Wales are strong but the orientation of the Welsh road network remains problematic for those who seek to develop the physical and cultural unity of Wales.

Roads are part of the complex recipe that makes up national identity. The landscape, architecture, and flora/fauna of motorways are no different in Wales than in England. Roads and driving, with their signage, rules and conventions, are a strong common experience across Britain, and part of the everyday practices that help sustain an assumed sense of national identity.

CROESO I GYMRU/WELCOME TO WALES

The sense of British integration that motorways help sustain is still within the confines of symbolic internal difference. Crossing a major bridge gives a sense of occasion to entering and leaving Wales. Moreover, once over the border, bilingual road signs are a visible symbol to visitors and locals that Wales has its own culture and identity, even if that is contained with a British system that demanded the signs have the same colour and design schemes as England.

The M4 does thus contribute to a sense of place. This may not be very specific because motorways are a blur of places passed by at speed by drivers focussing on the traffic around them. Instead, the meaning of motorways lies in their length and entirety rather than any specific spot. To travel down the M4 is to see South Wales. Everything from castles to country houses and steelworks to government office blocks are clearly visible, even to a driver concentrating on the road. On a wider level, the simple existence of the road changed people's mental perceptions of distance, even contributing to a sense that Wales itself was not so cut off from the wider world.

Yet familiarity with the road, weather, traffic conditions and the presence of passengers all vary the experience of travelling along the motorway. Commutes are integrated into the routines of people's individual lives, a time to think, listen to music or talk. Landmarks can have specific meanings for individuals, a marker of how far it is to home or the place that a child always jokes about.

But these are relatively minor differences and still exist within the confines of the road itself and the traffic controls and customs that govern how a motorway is travelled. The M4 thus still became embedded in many people's perception of the region they lived in or visited, a common experience and place that helped them understand what South Wales was.

GETTING FROM ONE PLACE TO ANOTHER

Most of the population of South Wales must have used the M4 at some point. Indeed, it made it possible to live in one place but work some distance away. Yet people rarely think of its impact on Wales, except perhaps in communities where the road changed their character, whether that was the physical, aesthetic and sensory intrusion of an urban stretch or how being located near an exit transformed quiet rural villages or suburbs into commuter belts.

The harmful rather than liberating effect of transport might most obviously be true for those who lived in the way of or near new roads but motorways also have environmental consequences that affect everyone. But until the late 1970s such environmental concerns were marginal voices and even now the pollution and physical intrusion of the road across the South Wales landscape is normally considered secondary to the economic benefits of easier travel. It could be decades before we appreciate the true environmental cost of the dependency on cars that emerged in the 1950s, 1960s and 1970s.

But few would want to go back to a time when travelling across South Wales meant crawling along at a snail's pace. The motorway is part of a host of technological changes that have made life easier. Simply getting from one place to another is now quicker, smoother and less frustrating that ever before. And for that reason alone the M4 is one of the most important places in the history of Wales.

Further Reading:
Joe Moran, *On Roads. A Hidden History* (2009)

194

23

THE WELSH ASSEMBLY BUILDING, CARDIFF BAY

Andrew Edwards

Type 'most iconic building' into an internet search engine and it will come up with the expected array of candidates; the Empire State Building, the Eiffel Tower, Big Ben, the Taj Mahal: the list is endless and impressive. We could debate at some length which one of these (and many others) merits the claim to be *the* most iconic (the Pyramids seem a particular favourite of internet geeks) and, no doubt, a case could be made for the inclusion of some Welsh landmarks in a 'top 100'. Rugby aficionados may well make a case for the Millennium Stadium, whilst some of the many castles, bridges and historic monuments which constitute our national treasures may also be worth a shout; but nothing in Wales come close to the Welsh Assembly building in deserving the status as Wales's most important, and iconic, building.

Buildings don't necessarily have to be old to be iconic, and it is often said that some things in life are worth waiting for. If this is true, then the people of Wales showed a remarkable degree of patience waiting for the construction of this particular building. As is often the case with iconic buildings, the Welsh Assembly has a controversial past. Some activists spent a lifetime campaigning for it. Some people in Wales didn't want to see it built. Others would, no doubt, gladly drive a bulldozer through it today. The road which led to the construction of the Welsh Assembly was long and difficult. The often divisive and bitter debates over devolution which spanned more than a century exposed social, geographic, cultural and linguistic differences between people living in Wales. The case for and against the Assembly highlighted the fact that for 'the Welsh', identity and politics were often hotly contested and problematic issues.

CAMPAIGNS FOR AN ASSEMBLY

In the modern era, the battles for self-government can be traced back to the ultimately unsuccessful but inspirational Cymru Fydd (Young Wales) campaigns of the 1880s and 1890s. In the immediate aftermath of the First World War, further discussions of devolution (seen at the time as a means of lessening the burden on an overstretched Westminster) also came to nothing and Wales had to wait until the 1950s for another serious discussion of self-government, this time via the Liberal/Nationalist 'Parliament for Wales' campaign of the early 1950s. In the 1960s, Harold Wilson's Labour government (having appointed the first Secretary of State for Wales in 1964) also considered devolution for Wales as a means of reforming the machinery of government but, fearful that devolution would be a sop to nationalism, appointed a Royal Commission to investigate constitutional change. Following the publication of a positive Commission report in 1973 and evidence of further Labour erosion at the hands of Scottish (and to a lesser extent Welsh) nationalism in the general election of February 1974, devolution returned to the political agenda in Labour's October 1974 election manifesto.

However, despite being a Labour manifesto commitment, the battle for devolution in the late 1970s will best be remembered for the 'no' campaign led by the party's renegade 'gang of six' Welsh MPs which included, most

Harold Wilson, whose 1960s Labour government considered devolution for Wales

prominently, Neil Kinnock, and Leo Abse. Although the activities of the 'no' campaign certainly had an impact in the scale of defeat, the reality was – as opinion polls throughout the period consistently highlighted – that devolution was dead in the water long before the infamous referendum of 1 March 1979, when only one in five Welsh voters supported the measure. Wales had to wait another eighteen years for another chance to support devolution and, in the referendum of September 1997, Welsh voters endorsed the Labour government's proposals by the narrowest of margins.

The debates over devolution tended to centre around the rationale for self-government and on the relative merits of the 'pro' and 'anti' case rather than what a Welsh Parliament, Government, Senate or Assembly (all were fashionable titles at one time or another) would look like. When discussions over a building did take place, they tended to focus on pragmatic issues including the cost and especially the location of an Assembly and both, especially the location of an Assembly, were highly contentious issues.

THE LOCATION OF THE ASSEMBLY

Tucked away in a quiet corner of Cardiff Bay, the Assembly building looks out over the waters that once dispatched coal to the four corners of the globe. Close to the trendy bars, restaurants and shops in the revamped hub of industrial Cardiff, it is sometimes hard to imagine the rugged, tough and uncompromising industrial world that once existed and thrived there 'when coal was king'. Of course 'old Wales' passed away some time ago. It was therefore unsurprising that many saw the arrival of devolution and the opening of the Assembly as marking the arrival of a 'new Wales' and also appropriate that the new Assembly building should end up being erected close to the hub of old industrial Wales.

But finding a new home for the Assembly was never straightforward. Just after the First World War conferences on devolution exposed the difficulties of finding a home for an Assembly. Representatives from North Wales feared that an Assembly located in the south would be disadvantageous, since it would be as remote (in geographical as well as political terms) as Westminster. Rural representatives from mid Wales made the same point, fearing that an Assembly based in an urban centre would inevitably be dominated by the concerns of the densely populated industrial heartlands. At that point at least, it was far from inevitable that an Assembly would be located in South Wales and some suggested that there should perhaps be two Assemblies, one in the south and one in the north, as a means of addressing the problem. Other towns also made a case for housing an Assembly. Llandrindod Wells – a town which incidentally hosted one of the post-war conferences on devolution in 1919 – was also seen as a convenient halfway house between North and South Wales. Aberystwyth was touted as a possible location for the Assembly due to its location in neutral mid Wales. Machynlleth also presented a powerful case, not least because it had been the location for the seat of Owain Glyndwr's Welsh Parliament back in 1404 and held the unofficial status as the ancient capital of Wales. There were other northern claims for an Assembly to be located in Caernarfon (for historic) and Wrexham (for pragmatic) reasons.

However, as early as the 1920s, the momentum had already begun to swing in the direction of Cardiff, as it became the most prominent Welsh administrative centre, housing the offices of civil servants charged with safeguarding Welsh interests in issues including health and education. By the end of the Second World War, Cardiff was also widely regarded as the capital city of Wales, and official status was confirmed in 1955. By 1964, Cardiff's future case was further strengthened when the newly established Welsh Office made its home in Cathays Park.

By the 1970s, when the Labour government announced its plans for devolution, there was again no great vision for an Assembly building. Pro-devolutionists talked of the costs of *establishing* an Assembly, but (in part because of the need to keep costs low) there were few references to a new and symbolic building. However, it was clear that Cardiff was the expected destination. The home of the new Assembly was to be the Coal Exchange built in Cardiff Bay in the 1880s, famously the location of the first recorded million-pound business deal back in 1901. Pro-devolution campaign leaflets in the late 1970s hailed 'Cardiff's magnificent Coal Exchange – helping to breathe new life into the traditional heart of our capital city'.

The rest, as they say, is history. Convinced, in part at least, by the arguments of anti-devolutionists, Welsh voters rejected devolution by a thumping majority and we had to wait until 1997 for devolution to arrive. As had been the case in the 1970s, it was again assumed that the Assembly would be located in Cardiff, though this time Cardiff City Hall rather than the Coal Exchange was touted as its likely destination. However, a consultative document produced by the Welsh Office shortly after the arrival of devolution set out a shortlist of possible sites and these included a North Wales location (Wrexham), as well as Swansea Guildhall and a site in Cardiff Bay where a new building could be erected (although the economic benefits for housing the Assembly ensured that bids also came in from other parts of Wales).

Swansea's case for housing the new Assembly was particularly strong since it, unlike Cardiff, had actually voted in favour of devolution in 1997 and it also seemed to carry support from other parts of the country where it was feared that devolution would do much for Cardiff, but little for the rest of Wales. However, despite the legitimate pragmatic, sentimental or historic claims of other towns and cities, the weight of historical precedent ensured that Cardiff would always be favourite in what turned out to be a two-horse race. Capital cities have traditionally been centres of administration and of government (though Bolivia, the Ivory Coast and the Netherlands provide just some exceptions to the rule) and it was no coincidence that Cardiff's campaign for the Assembly emphasized that it, not Swansea, was 'the established administrative and political heart of Wales' as well as its capital city.

A NEW BUILDING FOR A NEW NATION

Once it had been decided in 1998 that Cardiff Bay was the be the venue for a newly built Assembly, an international design competition was held to invite plans for the new building, with the Richard Rogers Partnership emerging as the winners. Built at a cost of £67 million, and unveiled by the Queen on 1 March 2006 the design of the Assembly was underpinned by a desire to ensure that

The building that marks the birth of a new Wales

the building generated the values and ambitions of a new government and, in a broader sense, a new nation. The lack of a detailed blueprint for the building was advantageous since it allowed architects to be creative and innovative with the design. Perhaps sensitive to the fears of devo-sceptics and the still strong anti-devolution lobby in Wales, the Assembly building was designed to display visibility, openness, democracy, transparency and innovation.

LOOKING IN AND OUT

The building was designed to allow the public to look in on the work of its elected representatives, but at the same time allowed those members to look out towards the wider world. The Assembly's circular Chamber was designed to facilitate a more open and inclusive democratic process and to act as a bulwark against the confrontational, adversarial and much derided Westminster model, and public galleries were also designed to allow full transparency of the Assembly's proceedings. There was also an eye to sustainable development. The ventilation, heating and lighting of the building were all designed to make best use of natural resources and to be environmentally sustainable (the roof, for example, collects the ample supply of Welsh rainwater which is then stored as the primary supply for the flushing of WC's as well as irrigation and maintenance).

LIVING UP TO EXPECTATIONS?

Back in the 1970s and 1990s some opponents of devolution evoked doomsday scenarios if the Welsh Assembly ever came into being. As the late Labour MP for Pontypool Leo Abse once eloquently put it, the Welsh Assembly would do for Wales what 'Brains Brewery would do for alcoholics'. Conservative MPs suggested that the opening of an Assembly would be like supplying 'opium to disenchanted Celts'. In the north, opponents suggested that the Assembly would be dominated by a corrupt southern Labour mafia; in the south there were fears that it would become the (Welsh) language obsessed fortress of culturally-minded nationalists. Neil Kinnock was among those who argued that money spent on an Assembly building would be better spent building new schools and hospitals in Wales. Back in 1997, another fear was that the Assembly would be overrun by 'second-rate glorified county councillors'. Even supporters of devolution have, at times, expressed concern that the quality of debates behind the impressive façade of the Assembly building have failed to live up to expectations.

Yet, the new Assembly building has already witnessed some striking and positive advancements. Back in the dark days of the 1980s, few would have envisaged a Welsh Conservative party positively engaging with the devolution process and constructing an agenda with a distinctively Welsh flavour for the

The Senedd building in Cardiff Bay

first time in over half a century. Few still would have conceived of a government where power was shared between Plaid Cymru and Labour. In the male-dominated Welsh political jungle of the 1970s an Assembly where women would play such a prominent role was also unimaginable. We are also, slowly, becoming more conscious of the importance of the Assembly. Successive opinion polls have demonstrated that support for the Assembly has grown steadily over recent years and the positive outcome of the recent referendum on extending the powers of the Assembly shows that the people of Wales are slowly warming to devolution.

WALES WITHOUT THE ASSEMBLY?

When the Assembly was being designed, another remit for the architects was that the building was not lavish. Drive into Cardiff and the steel structure of the Millennium Stadium catches the eye: the Assembly building is nowhere to be seen and, for first-time visitors to Cardiff, it can take a bit of finding. Especially compared to many of its older European counterparts the Welsh Assembly is a modest building. In some respects it represents some of our positive national characteristics. The Assembly is not big, bold and brash (you can draw your own conclusions as to which European nations fit these particular criteria). Like the Wales of old, it is small, modest and unassuming. But like the new Wales it is at the same time smart, modern and dynamic.

Some in Wales may still like to see a fleet of bulldozers descending on Cardiff Bay tasked with tearing it down. There may still be claims for an Assembly to be situated away from Cardiff in a more neutral venue (though the Assembly has now spawned siblings across Wales in an effort to address some of these concerns). It will, no doubt, witness some notable failures as well as successes over the next hundred years. It will also be inhabited from time to time by representatives who will disappoint. However, the Assembly building is the cornerstone of a new, increasingly autonomous, and self-reliant Wales. Evidence clearly suggests that the majority of us (amongst us many who voted 'no' in 1979 and 1997) no longer wish to see Wales without an Assembly. Two buildings in Cardiff carry the name 'Millennium' (the Stadium, opened in 1999 and Centre, opened in 2004), but neither marks the dawn of a new century and the birth of a new Wales more than the Welsh Assembly building.

Further Reading

K. Morgan and K. Mungham, *Redesigning Democracy: The making of the Welsh Assembly* (2000)

24

A BEATING HEART IN WELSH HISTORY – SOCCER GROUNDS

H. V. Bowen

A bold marketing campaign has been boasting that rugby union lies at the 'heart of the nation'. A recruitment drive invites us to 'join the beat' and take an active role in the 'national sport of Wales'. As guardians of their game, the Welsh Rugby Union has a perfect right to say whatever it likes. And it has to be applauded for its efforts to stimulate grass roots involvement in sport. But it is always important that we cast a critical eye over the claims of any organisation that is brazen enough to appropriate 'the nation' and then position itself at its very heart.

'NATIONAL SPORTS': WHICH SPORTS, WHOSE IDENTITY?

A discussion centred on identifying 'the national sport' of any country is usually a futile and pointless exercise. Much depends on definitions and who exactly is having the discussion. One thing is for sure, though, and that is that in a sporting sense all nations have many beating hearts, and Wales is no different. If we avert our glaze from our sporting navel for a moment and look beyond the Millennium Stadium, we will find hearts beating in many buildings and places across Wales: from beaches to snooker halls, mountains to boxing rings; swimming pools to cycle tracks.

It would be foolish in the extreme to deny that, over the last century or so, rugby union has become bound up in a particular version of Welsh national identity and indeed self-identity. But identities are complicated things and when they lazily translate into simplistic images and slogans they serve only to disrespect, disenfranchise, and alienate those who do not conform to a particular stereotype. It is important, then, that before any game is placed at the 'heart of the nation' we would do well to remember that very large numbers of people don't have the faintest interest in it at all, let alone ever want to participate in it.

To be fair, rugby union does still capture the attention of people across Wales during the Six Nations tournament or during a successful World Cup campaign, when a media-driven frenzy can whip some of us into a state of great excitement, bordering on mass hysteria.

Indeed, the *Western Mail* should at this point take a bow for its exhaustive and exhausting urgings to us to get behind 'the boys'. But after the Grand Slam celebrations and hangovers have subsided; after we have all put away our inflatable leeks and daffodil headgear for another time; and after we have taken out yet another mortgage so that we can buy tickets again next year, there is, in the cold light of day, an alternative perspective to be offered on the self-styled 'national sport of Wales'.

THE STRANGE DEATH OF WELSH RUGBY

It might be suggested that, in some ways, rugby union football is not, and never has been, the national sport of Wales. No more so has this been the case than at present, as before our very eyes the regional and club game continues to wither away at an alarming pace.

Many of the great rugby grounds of Wales are now crumbling mausoleums, sad reminders of former times when great clubs were vibrant and densely populated parts of the communities in which they were located. Pontypool Park, The Brewery Field, St Helen's, to name but three. In many parts of Wales, rugby union is now experiencing a slow, painful, and very strange death, at the very moment that the national team is carrying all before it in Europe.

Of course, at the depths of a nasty and sustained economic recession, people's discretionary spending decisions will always be affected, and this in part explains poor attendances at all levels of the game. But there is more to it than that.

The reorganisation of the game in Wales over the last ten years has undoubtedly helped to produce an exciting national side, now touted as being one of the best ever. But this has come at a great social cost, as many of the historic links between communities and the top-level game have been severed. Beyond the national team, the top-level game has retreated to the South Wales coastal strip where oddly or blandly named 'regions' such as

A view of the Vetch

the Ospreys or Blues now play out their important Heineken Cup fixtures in echoing new stadia that are less than one-third full.

Yet at other times those grounds are bursting at the seams as Cardiff City and Swansea City strut their entertaining stuff before raucous capacity crowds of more than 20,000 people. Nowadays, the hottest tickets in Wales are not for the Welsh rugby union team, but for the Cardiff City Stadium and the Liberty Stadium when the Bluebirds and the Swans are playing at home.

THE PEOPLE'S GAMES: WHICH PEOPLE?

It is instructive more generally to compare rugby union with association football or 'soccer' as it has always been known in Wales. The latest International Rugby Board figures suggest that in Wales there are now 314 rugby union clubs and a total of 79,800 registered and unregistered players (male and female).

By comparison, FIFA's official figures indicate that there are 1,920 soccer clubs in Wales with 173,550 registered and unregistered players. Such figures should be treated with a large pinch of salt (how on earth can unregistered players be counted?), but nonetheless the differences between the two codes are now very striking.

These figures should also not be surprising, because at grass roots level, and indeed at street level, soccer in Wales has often been in very rude good health. For example, over many decades the Swansea Senior League was one of the largest in the UK. And schoolboy sides from Wales were conspicuously successful in English schools competitions, no more so than the great Swansea sides of the 1930s, 1940s, and 1950s organised by the legendary Gabe Williams and Dai Beynon.

And, of course, unlike rugby grounds, soccer grounds are to be found in all corners of Wales, in almost every town and village. Sets of rugby posts have always been absent from many places in mid and North Wales. If you don't believe me then have a look when you next cross the country by rail or road.

The Bluebirds have flown their old nest at Ninian Park

It is important, then, that we recognise that strong beating hearts have always been found in the soccer grounds of Wales, and these grounds have contributed to the making of their own distinctive form of national identity.

For many years Newport County and Wrexham flew the Welsh flag alongside Cardiff and Swansea in the English Football League, and they were joined briefly by Aberdare and Merthyr during the inter-war years. This meant that Ninian Park, Vetch Field, Somerton Park, the Racecourse Ground, Penydarren Park, and Aberdare Athletic Ground all helped to add a distinctively Welsh feel to Britain's 'national game'.

BELLE VUE AND STEBONHEATH

Other grounds have been of vital importance in the various manifestations of all-Wales Leagues that have existed over the years. There have been many of them: Farrar Road in Bangor, Belle Vue in Rhyl, Park Avenue in Aberystwyth, Stebonheath in Llanelli, and my own personal favourite, Y Traeth in Porthmadog. There are too many interesting grounds to list here, but they all have their own unique histories and have contributed to the development of Wales as a sporting nation.

One of world football's hottest properties, Cardiff-born Gareth Bale

VETCH FIELD: A 'RUBBLE HEAP' CRUCIBLE OF MODERN WELSH IDENTITY

Two points used to be made by those who objected to any claims that soccer had a prominent place in Welsh society.

They saw soccer (and perhaps still do) as being in many ways 'alien' to Wales, an imported proletarian game played by the unrespectable 'hooligan classes', conveniently overlooking the fact that rugby union originated in England and was brought into Wales by upper-middle class hooligan types in public schools such as Llandovery College.

They also saw soccer as offering a threat to Welsh culture because in many places it drew participation from English-speaking immigrants as both players and spectators. The newspapers of the 1920s and 1930s are replete with disparaging comments about the denizens of the 'dribbling code'.

But in fact soccer grounds in Wales facilitated a co-mingling of Welsh and English cultures, and at times they offered a heady mix of the traditional and the modern. No more so, perhaps, was this the case than at Vetch Field, home between 1912 and 2005 to Swansea Town/City.

The Vetch was an eccentrically constructed football ground wedged uncomfortably between tight, narrow streets of terraced housing. Overlooked by Townhill, and standing next to a Victorian prison 'way down by the sea', the

Vetch might charitably be considered to have been 'quaint'. Many thought it a dump, and it was once described as a 'rubble heap' of a ground.

But the great sporting journalist Frank Keating was perhaps rather closer to the mark when he penned a fond description of the Vetch as a 'variegated Heath Robinson cartoon'. 'Nowhere', he wrote, can 'Wales's inherent soccer culture be better evoked than in those paint-peeled stanchions at Swansea's Vetch.'

This curious home of the Swans saw great days and grim days; excitement and tedium; drama, tragedy, and more than a little farce. Some truly great football artists graced the Vetch; but over the years a rather greater number of plodding artisans plied their trade on the characteristically uneven, sloping playing surface.

Occasionally the sun shone; more often it seems to have rained. But throughout it all, the awkwardly positioned stands, banks, and terraces of the Vetch served to create a very special sporting arena, where successive generations of supporters gave expression to the joys and despairs of following the fluctuating fortunes of 'the Swans'.

Before the modern age of the purpose-built all-seater sports stadia boasting corporate facilities, bars, restaurants, and conference suites, the establishment of football grounds in Britain was mostly unplanned and haphazard. Sites were acquired and cleared; then proper grass playing-surfaces were created, together with small pavilions or wooden grandstands for the well-to-do; before, finally, rudimentary viewing facilities were provided for large numbers of working-class spectators in the form of raised 'banks'. Early grounds thus evolved in piecemeal fashion, often coming into being in a matter of weeks and then evolving only very slowly over a number of decades.

No more so was this the case than in Swansea where, in bold defiance of the basic laws of geometry and common sense, a football ground was somehow wedged awkwardly into the triangular communal space that represented the only large and open area of flat land anywhere near the centre of the town.

By making a home for their club at 'Vetch Field', the pre-First World War pioneers of professional football in Swansea created a sporting home whose physical location dictated that its architectural characteristics were thereafter to be defined by sharp angles, broken lines, and complete lack of any sense of symmetry. Indeed, there could be no greater contrast than between the chaotic jumble of the Vetch Field ground, and the clean shape, metallic shine, and perfect dimensions of the new Liberty Stadium.

It is, however, somehow appropriate that Swansea's major football ground was created on a site squeezed between the County Jail, the Royal Arsenal,

Hancock's Brewery, and the Salvation Army Barracks, all of which were to provide various forms of comfort and services for several generations of Swans' fans.

At the same time, the fact that the Vetch Field was bordered by the terraced houses and back yards of Glamorgan Street, William Street, Gam Street, and Little Madoc Street meant that Swansea Town almost literally carved out a place for itself at the very heart of the local community in the Sandfields area of the town. Again, there is a marked contrast with the new stadium which stands in splendid isolation on a reclaimed copper-slag heap on the banks of the River Tawe.

During the early years at the Vetch, the supporters gave noisy backing to their team, and in doing so they revealed much about who they were and who they thought they were. In 1926 it was said that 'ordinarily the cheering can be heard as far as Fforestfach', which was no mean feat even before the age of heavy noise pollution.

Those on the main Bank seem to have required little encouragement to strike up a song, and they often ran through a medley of popular hits and hymns, many of which were sung in Welsh. Thus the crowd often burst into

Schoolboys crane for a view at Ninian Park

spontaneous renditions of 'Cwm Rhondda', 'Mae Hen Wlad Fy Nhadau', 'Sosban Fach', and 'Yn y Dyfroedd Mawr a'r Tonnau'. When a visiting Stoke City supporter was told that the last hymn was usually heard at funerals, he looked shocked and then replied 'If that is so, then we had better hum "Show me the way to go home."'

The enthusiastic singing of such hymns and arias certainly gave a distinctive Welsh feel to big games at the Vetch, but while the crowd were giving vocal expression to a form of Welshness, they cannot be said to have used the game of football to make any wider or deeper political points about nationalism or national identity. As is always the case, most were only ninety-minute nationalists, but they certainly enjoyed participating in mass community singing.

CHICK-CHICK-CHICKEN

The Vetch crowd also took up English-language popular tunes with equal enthusiasm, especially in the case of 'I'm forever blowing bubbles' and 'Danny Boy'. Indeed, with just a little creative imagination a hit song was soon adapted to celebrate the scoring prowess of the marauding centre-forward Jack Fowler. 'Chick, chick, chick, chick, chicken, lay a little egg for me' was reworded to become 'Fow, Fow, Fow, Fow, Fowler, score a little goal for me, We haven't had a goal since the last match and now it's half past three'.

Tapping into this crowd participation, the club often encouraged the Vetch voices to stretch their musical chords even further. At the Bury FA Cup tie in 1927 mass singing was organised at a game in Wales for the first time when the conductor Thomas Radcliffe led the crowd through a repertoire of popular numbers. The ground, it was said, 'blossomed into song', and 'the harmony and melody of community singing rose on the fog-laden air.'

Later, records were played over the PA system in order to get the crowd going, although this did not always have the desired effect. At the Portsmouth Cup tie of 1934 hit tunes were played 'but a big section of the crowd preferred Welsh hymns and particularly "Cwm Rhondda"'. Contrary to popular belief in some quarters, such hymns have never been the exclusive property of rugby union crowds.

SOCCER GROUNDS AND WELSHNESS

Almost exactly the same points and evidence that apply to the Vetch could be used in relation to the other soccer grounds of Wales. In different ways they all helped to create a form of culture that was different from that which developed in grounds where rugby union was played. It was a culture that was no better or worse than rugby culture, but it offered, and continues to offer, people the opportunity to express alternative versions of Welshness. And 'the beat' of the heart to be found in these grounds is very strong indeed. That is why the soccer grounds of Wales matter, and why they deserve a very prominent place in Welsh history.

Further reading:
Daryl Leeworthy, *Fields of Play: The Sporting Heritage of Wales* (2012)

Notes on Contributors

 David Austin is Professor of Archaeology at University of Wales Trinity St David.

 Robin Barlow is Higher Education Advisor, Recruitment and Admissions, at Aberystwyth University.

 H.V. Bowen is Professor of Modern History at Swansea University and Convenor of History Research Wales.

 Lloyd Bowen is Senior Lecturer in Early Modern and Welsh History at Cardiff University.

 Andy Croll in Principal Lecturer in History at the University of South Wales.

 Ben Curtis is Research Associate at Aberystwyth University and a History Tutor at the Centre of Lifelong Learning at Cardiff University.

 Andrew Edwards is Senior Lecturer in Modern History at Bangor University.

 Chris Evans is Professor of History at the University of South Wales.

 Madeleine Gray is Reader in History at University of South Wales.

 Ray Howell is Professor of Welsh Antiquity at the University of South Wales.

 Martin Johnes is Senior Lecturer in History at Swansea University.

Bill Jones is Professor in Modern Welsh History at Cardiff University.

Raimund Karl is Professor of Archaeology and Heritage at Bangor University.

Iwan Rhys Morus is Professor of History at Aberystwyth University.

Helen J. Nicholson is Reader in History at Cardiff University.

Paul O'Leary is Senior Lecturer in Welsh History at Aberystwyth University.

Lowri Ann Rees is Lecturer in Modern History at Bangor University.

Andrew Richardson is Postgraduate Pathways Project Officer at Cardiff University.

Steven Thompson is Senior Lecturer in Modern History at Aberystwyth University.

Peter Wakelin is Head and Chief Executive Officer of the Royal Commission on the Ancient and Historical Monuments of Wales.

Chris Williams is Professor of Welsh History and Director of the Research Institute for Arts and Humanities at Swansea University.

Alun Withey, formerly Lecturer in History at Swansea University, is now Associate Research Fellow at the University of Exeter.

Martin Wright is Lecturer in History (Welsh Medium) at Cardiff University.

David Wyatt is Lecturer in Early Medieval History, Community and Engagement at Cardiff University.